I AM JUN JILV, AND SO ARE YOU!

Thoughts from a Tiny Human on Living a Giant Life

by
Anjali Bhimani

The information in this book was correct at the time of publication, but the Author does not assume any liability for loss or damage caused by errors or omissions.

Copyright © 2022 by Anjali Bhimani

All rights reserved. No part of this book may be reproduced or used in any manner without the prior written permission of the copyright owner, except for the use of brief quotations in a book review.

To request permission, contact the publisher at info@tinypawspublishing.com.

Edited by Lauren Terrell, Chantel Hamilton, and Jessica Sherer
Cover Art and Illustrations by Vivian Truong
Cover Design and Layout by Sandy Kreps

ISBN: 979-8-9865342-0-6

CONTENTS

Foreword 9

Helllooooooooooo! 13

    Your Guide on Today's Tour 14

    The I Am Fun Size Origin Story 18

    How to Use This Book 28

    The Struggle is Real (Seriously) 31

The Fun Size Hero's Journey 36

Part 1: In the Beginning 41

    Panic at the ~~Disco~~ Starting Line 42

    Charley Lesson #1: Mama, Chill 46

    Choose Your Own New Year (as Many Times as You Want)! 48

    Jeannie Bolet 51

    Ready! Set! Wait....Where Am I Going Again? 52

    Are You Running From Something or Running To Something? 57

    Discipline Is Deciding 61

    It's Just Do It, Not Just Share It 69

    Just Because You Can Have It All Doesn't Mean You Have To 73

    Charley Lesson #2: More Toys All At Once Does Not Equal More Fun 78

Choosing the Perfect Path 80

Jennifer Hale 84

My Favorite Answer 85

When It's Good to Be Bad at Something 91

Only You Decide Who You Are 97

Crispin Freeman 103

Charley Lesson #3: If You Listen, I Will Tell You What I Need 104

How the Hell Do I Love Myself? 106

The Candy-Coated Shell 112

Mela Lee 117

Enjoying the Quest 118

Jason Ritter 121

Don't Forget to Play 125

Part 2: The Messy Middle 129

When Life Happens… 130

What You Resist…Punches You in the Fucking Face 136

A Quick Reminder to Put on Your Oxygen Mask First 142

Charley Lesson #4: It's Time for CharleyBall! 148

Is It Rejection or Projection? 150

Knowing Your Worth 154

Cara Theobold 161

A Space Opera Trilogy (Sort Of) 162

My Secret to Staying Positive All the Time 176

Thoughts on Loneliness 179

Who's in Your Head? 182

Charley Lesson #5: You Know What Would Make Us Both Feel Better? 186

Melanie Stone 188

Are You Inspiring or In-spiral-ing? 189

Fabulous FOMO 195

Carolina Ravassa 201

Regaining Faith in Yourself After Tough Times 202

Give the Pain a Purpose 209

Whatever the Weather 217

Josh Petersdorf 221

Part 3: The Home Stretch 223

How to Get Over Underestimating Yourself 224

Jen Cohn 236

Touchstones, Silly Songs, and Good Mornings 237

I'm So Nervous (or Am I?) 251

Your Personal Superpower 257

Celebrate Where You Are 260

Caroline Kinsolving 266

We Are All Artists 268

Savoring the Simple Moments 274

Charley Lesson #6: Focus Up, Mama 278

Cultivating Wonder (Thank You, Ms. Huffington) 280

Chloe Hollings 288

There Is No Wasted Time 289

Wait a Second. Is This...Happiness? 297

Elle Newlands 296

Some Final Thoughts (Just for Now...) 301

Acknowledgements 305

Notes 308

About the Author 310

To Rick, my forever rock star, onstage and off;

To Mom, Dad, and Anish for teaching me to feel big, love hard, and be myself (and for not strangling me as a teenager, although you probably wanted to);

To Nick and Bella for giving me more reasons every day to be better at life and to lead by example;

To Cathleen for helping me reach for the stars with my feet on the ground;

To Raj for reminding me to live life artfully;

To Charley Boo for picking me as your mama;

To the incredibly generous, talented, and supportive online community who inspired this book;

And to the Kickstarter backers who made it possible without taking out a second mortgage on our home:

This is for all of you.

Love,
Me

FOREWORD

"I take my fun seriously."

Anjali said this on the very first day I met her at an *Overwatch* meet-up on Blizzard campus back in 2016. I believe she has said it every time I have seen her since. You will, in fact, read about this quippy mantra in this very book you are holding! The first time I heard this catchphrase, I thought, "This is a woman who knows exactly what she wants."

But over the years of knowing Anjali, I've come to realize it goes far beyond being certain in oneself—it is much deeper than that. In fact, every time I hear those five words, it means something different to me in each moment; I'm left with a different takeaway that echoes in my mind until the next time those words enter my brain. Reading through this book gave me a similar feeling.

Confession time: I'm not a huge fan of self-help books. I often find them, dare I say, pretentious, and written from a deeply removed and often outdated perspective of what the average person is going through while on this wild rollercoaster we commonly refer to as "life." Every clause on how to "simply reframe your thinking" or "alter your perspective" often provokes my inner angsty teenager that wants to loudly defend herself with a snappy, "You don't know me!"

But, not more than a page into this book, I found myself sinking into my chair, relaxing as I giggled and nodded along to Anjali's intoxicating exuberance towards life. I quickly lost track of time, and a quarter of the way through the book, it hit me: This just feels like hanging out with Anjali!

In my darkest times, my first instinct isn't to pick up a self-help book. No, no, that sounds like the worst type of homework—the kind where you have to work on yourself. If I had to guess, my first instinct when I'm feeling my lowest is similar to many others: I pick up the phone and call my friends. That's what reading these pages evokes.

Craving those creature-comforts in times of need is the most basic of instincts, and what's more comforting than wrapping yourself in the warmth and compassion of those who love you most? In those moments after leaving many tears on a friend's shoulder, inevitably, a joke is made. And just like that, the tone shifts to laughter. Joy. *Fun*. After all, how else are you to regain control over the uncontrollable turmoil the universe throws at you?

Very few people make me feel as seen as Anjali. Her words tend to cut through even the thickest layers of armor. "I take my fun seriously," she told me on the set of a tabletop

RPG show I was producing. It's not uncommon for me to get so caught up in the usual stress of my job that I lose sight of the absurd reality that I get to play and create cool art with my friends for a living. I chuckled as I marked off another box on the running Anjali-bingo-card in my head. She took note and quickly responded, "Really! If I am going to spend the majority of my time working, it had better be fun. Life is too short for it not to be. This is serious fun."

The gravity of this moment will stick with me for the rest of my days. It finally clicked on what "I take my fun seriously" means to *me*. Anjali is an incredibly talented and successful person. She could've chosen to spend her time doing any number of things, but she chose to spend her valuable time with us, playing games while simultaneously exploring the deeper levels of the human experience.

Taking your fun seriously isn't about select occasions when you allow yourself revelry. It's about finding the revelry wherever you go, and encouraging it in others whenever you can—whether in work, in play, and yes, even in times of sadness. More than anyone I know, Anjali is an expert at siphoning every ounce of pure life from every moment she can, to its fullest extent.

So, take her hand. Let her show you her ways and be the shining beacon in your life like she has to many others, myself included. Whether you're in the darkest of times, or simply looking for little ways to audition better habits in your day-to-day life, grab a cup of coffee and have a little chat with Anjali. It's time to take off the wrapper, and dig into your "Fun Size" life!

> *~Marisha Ray – Creative Director and Founding Member, Critical Role Studios**

*Also Anjali's designated patron saint of gaming, badass boss lady, brilliant actress, and fellow loving dog mom

HELLLOOOOOOOOOOOOO!

I can't tell you how happy, honored, and grateful I am that you picked up this book. We're about to take a journey together, and I'm very excited to be walking beside you on it. It's your journey, the Fun Size Hero's Journey, if you will (with love and admiration to Joseph Campbell).

If you are in a dark place, take my hand for a little bit and let me turn on this flashlight in the cave. We can sit together or get up and walk out of it together, we can laugh together or you can cry on my shoulder while you read. If you're in the light, wonderful! Let's play a little more through these pages and see how much more we can help you squeeze from the game of life. Regardless of where you are or where you think you're stuck, you're in the right place. We're going to have some fun.

YOUR GUIDE ON TODAY'S TOUR...

While I'm slightly loathe to start the book by talking about myself because this is so much more about *you* than me, the chances are pretty high that you don't actually know who I am and just picked up this book because there was a dog wearing a cape on the cover. (That isn't a judgment. On the contrary, I think that's an *excellent* reason to have picked up this book. I insisted that Charley Dog have that cape, and I stand by the decision.)

I do think you should probably know who your tour guide is on this little adventure, though. (No, it's not Charley, although that introduction is coming, too.) So, let me just fill you in on a few fun facts about me that might be useful along the way:

My name is Anjali Bhimani. Hi! I pronounce my name AHN-juh-lee. Some others of Indian heritage may pronounce it differently, but this is the way I do it. It sounds not unlike the rather pungent "French" perfume, Enjoli, from the early '80s with the incredible commercial that's so bad it's good. (Look it up on YouTube. It's worth it.)

According to my beautiful and spiritual mother, my name means "a gift to God," which she says she chose for me because you offer what you most value to the divine—whatever divine tradition you believe in—as a sign of your devotion. Personally, I often joke that she chose it because she wanted to send me back, but there were no returns (har har).

Friends call me Anj, and you can, too, new friend. In high school, my nickname was "Sweet Anj," lovingly hollered at me with an elongated "eee," hence my social media handle, which drives grammarians a bit mad now and then, just like the title of this book. But what can I say? I'm just a spelling rebel.

I've spent a good 25 years of my life in a career as a professional actress. (For you more cynical folks out there, no, not a waitress; people in the service industry have infinitely more patience than I do and deserve a medal for their work every day.) I've been fortunate enough to perform in almost every medium that I can think of—theatre, dance, musicals, television, opera, film, video games, animation, motion capture, live role-playing game entertainment—and I'm always looking for more branches of the creative tree to swing from because I love storytelling more than I can possibly tell you. I believe that sharing stories—fictional, historical, and personal—is one of the most important ways we connect and help each other in this life. The second someone starts a sentence with "You know what you should do…" I tune out, but if it starts with "I remember this time when…" I lean in. Connection.

My spiritual and personal beliefs straddle the worlds of woo-woo and straight science, so you'll hear me refer to the Universe a lot while you'll also hear me dive into scientific explanations for what makes us and the world around us tick. Head in the stars, feet on the ground, that's how I like to be.

I am incredibly stubborn and independent (much to the alternating delight and chagrin of my husband, Rick, who you'll hear me refer to a lot in these pages; he is my rock and my rockstar, a world-class musician and a universe-class human), which means the worst way to get me to do what you want is to tell me what I can and can't do. When it comes to self-help books, lifehacks, guides on manifesting or self-care, or whatever, I am a firm believer in deciding what works best for me, and that everyone should get to do the same. So, please, you do you. (We'll get into this more later.)

I curse. A lot. Once when I was at a formal event with some friends, one of the gals turned to me and, upon seeing me dressed to the nines, said, "Anjali! You look so elegant! Don't open your mouth," to which I believe I replied, "Fuck that." Please know that for me it is not a form of disrespect but an active choice of how to convey a feeling. (I'd also like to think it's one thing that brings me closer to being like the incomparable Helen Mirren who has said publicly she tends to "swear like a potty-mouthed sailor."*)

I am the proud and endlessly grateful dog mom of the greatest pup in the world, a 12-pound Chihuahua-Pomeranian mix named Charley, aka Charley Boo,

*Interview in British *Vogue*, 2018

Helllooooooooooo!

Chartleby Barkenter, Biscuitologist, Charley Marbles, Carlos Maracas, Carlito Burrito, C Dawg, Paco the Taco, Buddy, Buddy Boo, and too many more names to count. I've learned so much since adopting this little bundle of greatness, so you'll hear about him (and see him depicted in the adorable art by Vivian Truong) a lot in this book. Go ahead and check out his cuteness on Instagram at @charleythebestdog. You won't be disappointed.

Finally, the greatest accomplishment of my life is amassing the circle of incredible people around me who have chosen to be in my life and let me into theirs—my friends and family. Indeed the line is so blurred between the two, it's odd to separate them. I am in awe of them every single day, and I'm so grateful for their constant willingness to accept me as I am but never settle for me being less than I can be. I owe so much to all of them, and I will never stop working to be worthy of their love and support.

Many of them have been guests on my YouTube series, and you'll get to read some nuggets of their absolute brilliance throughout this book. If I could have my entire circle on *I Am Fun Size*, I would (and I will keep adding more of them to the series as they become available), but for now, I hope you enjoy their love and support and wisdom as much as I do when you "meet" them in these pages.

Enough about me, let's talk about *you*. Since you're the reason this book exists.

The "I Am Fun Size" Origin Story

"A long time ago, in a galaxy far, far away..."

No, wait. Sorry. Wrong origin story.

Long ago, probably back as far as 2014 (yes, ye olde tyme), I toyed with the idea of creating a blog or website or something similar that would be of service to a community I belonged to but I didn't know which to choose or where to begin. I was leaning toward something of use to the petite females of the world, and I'd thought of plenty of ideas: fashion tips, inspirational writing, lifehacks for how to handle a world built for tall people (which for me was anyone over 5'5").

But despite my excellent hot tips for we the vertically challenged, I resisted pursuing it, knowing that somewhere, someone was going to feel left out. Or worse, demoralized. I wanted to do something for everyone, or at least, something for anyone who wanted to be a part of it. (The hesitation may also have come from my lifelong aversion to elimination games. If we're playing a game, why would we want to "knock someone out" of playing? I mean, dodgeball is downright inhumane.) That funny sixth sense that it wasn't the right idea, combined with my obsession with perfectionism and an admitted lack of focus, kept me from making this amorphous project a reality.

It took a series of truly extraordinary events to jolt me out of inaction, to show me exactly why the idea I had wasn't quite the right fit.

The end of 2016 was an incredible time in the true sense of the word, one of those hyper-life times where so many truly life-altering events were happening all at once, it would have been deemed implausible by any TV or movie critic. It was also a time that by all rights should have left me in a state of extreme sadness, or at least emotional whiplash, but instead was filling me with wonder and a strange sense that something magical was brewing despite experiencing a deep, deep loss.

In the most concise manner I can put it (as the full story of this period in my life is one for another time and another book, and only with my family's blessing), within a period of about 35 days, I had celebrated one of the most beautiful Thanksgivings I can remember with my family, purchased a home with my boyfriend, accepted his proposal of marriage, and simultaneously (starting two days after that beautiful Thanksgiving) watched as my father's health plummeted at the hands of a heart condition he had battled for years. The two plotlines eventually culminated in a wedding ceremony at the foot of my father's hospital bed on New Year's Day and saying goodbye to him (at least on this earthly plane) less than 24 hours later.

Fortunately, my father had still been in good enough health earlier that year to witness the launch of *Overwatch*, a wildly successful video game I had played a role in, and to see his daughter, who had been so obsessed with Wonder Woman and superheroes as a child, portraying a powerful, beautiful, brilliant hero herself, only this time, one of Indian descent, so all the little girls just like her finally had a superheroine who looked like them.

Set in "a world worth fighting for," *Overwatch* was changing the landscape of video games with its diversity and outlook on the world, and the incredible community surrounding the game embraced us voice actors wholly and passionately. It was a point of pride for my father—several times over the months after the release of the game, he would tell me about how he was sharing pictures of the character I played, Symmetra, with friends and family and pointing out how his daughter had stepped into a role just like the ones she idolized as a child.

The days leading up to and including the moment of my father's passing changed my life in a way I could never have anticipated. Just as he had done all throughout his healthier years, my father faced this reality in a wildly loving way. For months, he had been preparing us and himself for this moment with so much love and grace. I cannot imagine anyone leaving the planet more elegantly. Days before his passing, he explained to a room full of his medical team and immediate family why he was ready to move on. "I have had such a beautiful life, beautiful wife, beautiful children. I'm content now. I don't need to be greedy," he said.

When he passed—in his bed, surrounded by his family—a ray of sunlight came beaming through the clouds outside his hospital window. I thank the stars I took a picture of it on my phone, because if I hadn't, to this day I wouldn't believe it had indeed been real. Sometime after his last breath, after finally letting go of his hand, I went to the bathroom, and I remember suddenly just *feeling* him, even more strongly than I had felt him in his weakened body moments earlier. I felt him say, "I'm good, Anju, don't worry about me. I'm good. You'll be good, too."

As *Overwatch* continued its success and my acting career suddenly took off in a new and exciting way, it felt like each new event, each extraordinary new person who came into my life, each moment of serendipity was happening at Dad's direction. During his lifetime, he was probably the most outwardly excited member of my family when it came to my choice of career path. So, although he wasn't on this planet to witness my success, wherever he was, I felt him watching me proudly, holding his favorite single malt scotch in one hand and conducting the people in my world with the other, as if each person or event that came into my world was an instrument playing in a passionate, tumultuous symphony.

It was amidst all these events that the online community (maaaaaaaybe with a little energetic push from my father) stepped into my whirlwind of emotions and gave me the motivation and direction I'd been lacking for so many years.

The month of January 2017 found me in a state of *doing* a lot but not feeling like I was *creating* a lot or providing much service to the world. I was stepping into a very busy time in my career, still grieving the loss of my father, and still experiencing this persistent feeling that I needed to connect to the world, to others, in a more meaningful way.

Even when I wasn't feeling useful in my own life, even when I was feeling somewhat stuck, I had always found connecting with others in need to be the best way to work through my own difficult moments. So I began connecting with the online gaming community—gamers, artists, dreamers, all—interacting with them in joy and celebration as close to one-on-one as possible through tweets and posts.

Then one night—February 2, 2017 to be precise—I decided to throw out how much I love fan art and ask people to post their pieces for a Fan Art Friday. I tweeted on a Thursday night, thinking it would probably take some time for people to see it and respond. "Maybe," I thought, "I'll wake up to a few fun pieces tomorrow."

Anjali Bhimani ✓
@sweeetanj

Hey guys! U know how much I  ur fanart so how about we start a #fanartfriday thread here this week? Share ur faves WITH the artist's link!

9:01 PM · Feb 2, 2017 · Twitter for Mac

> **EVEN WHEN I WASN'T FEELING USEFUL IN MY OWN LIFE, EVEN WHEN I WAS FEELING SOMEWHAT STUCK, I HAD ALWAYS FOUND CONNECTING WITH OTHERS IN NEED TO BE THE BEST WAY TO WORK THROUGH MY OWN DIFFICULT MOMENTS.**

The wave of art that followed within moments was incredible, but even more overwhelming was the emotional smack in the face I got as the pieces poured in. Here were these people of all different backgrounds and levels of artistic mastery putting out their offering without question, just for the joy of it. They rallied like a creative army, lobbing bomb after bomb after bomb of artistic love my way. And my first thought was, *I've been talking about being of service with a vlog or blog for years, but I'm just sitting on my ass. Look at all these beautiful people jumping to the call as soon as I posted. Who the hell am I to not be putting out my offering to this community when they are so generous and fearless for me and each other? I have to do something for them—right now. Fuck perfection.*

I whipped out my MacBook Pro, and recorded a very chill and poorly lit video explaining that I had created an email address for people to send me their questions for a new YouTube series. And then I waited. By the next morning, I already had 50 emails with incredible questions to ponder and to answer—not about characters or games or projects, but about *life*.

Right then and there, *I Am Fun Size* was born.*

"Okay, but Anj, why 'Fun Size'? Doesn't that mean, ya know, small? Like, candy bars and short people?"

I'd been using the term "fun size" to describe my petite stature in a lighthearted way for ages (as have other people), but suddenly, I couldn't get out of my head that we are *all* Fun Size. Capital F, capital S. We are all built for *fun*, for living big, beautiful lives no matter our size, gender, religion, location, income, favorite color, or favorite breakfast food. Our souls aren't limited to what our bodies look like or what they can (or can't) do.

Having been petite all my life, I'm very sensitive to the difference between *being* small and *feeling* small. Yes, I'm 5'0", but no one I've ever met would say I have a small personality. Still, there have been times in my life when I have *felt* small—insignificant, unseen, embarrassed of who I was or of some fundamental aspect of my personality, and incapable of living the big, beautiful life I saw others living (or at least, that's how it looked from the outside). Whether it was unsupportive voices in my orbit or the ones in my own head (usually a combination of both), feeling small took my big, beautiful life away with a false perception of what was possible for me. And I knew there were likely many people in my online community—and the world— who were feeling the same way. I knew these incredibly generous humans throwing love bombs my way needed some love coming back their way, too. So I created these little messages in the form of YouTube videos that would pop into people's feeds at random every few days or weeks to remind all those lovely humans that they are Fun Size and that they are meant to live a big, beautiful, *fun* life.

As of writing this, there are four years' worth of *I Am Fun Size* episodes out there (and by the time you have this book in your hot little hands, even more). Some are just me

---

*It's been pointed out to me many times that it should be *Sized* with an "-ed." After talking to several grammarians and looking it up in multiple ways online, I decided that it's my series, my book, my rules. I like Fun Size candy bars, so I chose Fun Size. Fun Size Three Musketeers and Fun Size Butterfingers make me very, very happy. And since my handle online is @sweeetanj with three e's (spelling be damned), I'm ruling that it's I Am Fun Size, just like the bag of Three Musketeers in my kitchen. But don't let that stop you from making it your own. Fun size, fun sized, I don't care either way. You just make it you.

alone chatting with viewers over the interwebs like we are in the same room. (Thank you, technology, for making that connection possible.) Others are with dear friends and acquaintances from the entertainment industry who have been kind enough to share their own wisdom and experience with me and the viewers. Some are minutes long, others are hours. But all are my attempt to lob love bombs back to this community—to *you*.

> **FEELING SMALL TOOK MY BIG, BEAUTIFUL LIFE AWAY WITH A FALSE PERCEPTION OF WHAT WAS POSSIBLE FOR ME. AND I KNEW THERE WERE LIKELY MANY PEOPLE IN MY ONLINE COMMUNITY - AND THE WORLD - WHO WERE FEELING THE SAME WAY.**

This book, dear reader, is just an extension of that wonderful mission that started that fateful February day when an online community made this 5'0", 98-pound scrappy Indian woman burst with gratitude and feel 100-feet tall. While I am in *no* way a mental health professional, psychologist, therapist, LCSW, licensed health coach, certified practitioner of NLP, EFT, reiki, or guru of any kind, the most valuable thing I have to offer the world is my own unique set of experiences—my failures, my successes, my past and current struggles, my ups and downs and diagonals—and what I've learned from them.

Some of my observations, most in fact, won't be shockingly new. There are many speakers and authors who have spoken and written eloquently on these issues, and I've referred to some of my favorites in this book. I don't pretend my viewpoint is somehow a brand new one. But I do know from loads of experience that it doesn't matter. You can hear something 10 times, 100 times, 1,000 times, and it doesn't sink in. All it takes is that one time with just a slightly different angle or perspective for it to stick. It just takes looking through the kaleidoscope and turning it one notch to see a completely different picture, to unlock a world of difference.

So here we are, taking that YouTube series to the page. I hope you find some inspiration, laughs, and new perspectives by seeing the world through my lens for a bit. I hope you, as the curator of your own life, will take what resonates for you and nothing more. As Dame Maggie Smith's character says in the *Second Exotic Marigold Hotel*, "I don't give advice, I give opinions." Or more accurately in this case, I share experiences. Take what you want and leave the rest.

Thanks for joining me on this ride.

HOW TO USE THIS BOOK

In short (ha ha, very punny), use it however ya damn well please.

There are all sorts of books out there that need to be read from cover to cover, in linear fashion. There are books that have very specific structures and exercises, very specific ways for you to go about reading them.

THIS IS NOT ONE OF THOSE BOOKS.

As much as I love a good game plan, this book has none of that. No one is walking the path you are walking. No one is living the life you are living. And ultimately, you get to be the person who makes all the choices, gets all the credit, and takes all the responsibility for whatever happens. So this book is more like a set of little essays or tidbits that offer a look at things in a slightly different way with a slightly different perspective, rather than something that seems prescriptive.

There are plenty of other books with systems and lists and protocols and workbooks and all sorts of things that will tell you how to do things. I'd just like to help you turn the kaleidoscope of life one notch in one direction or another to see some alternative ways of creating a big, beautiful, *fun* life that maybe you didn't see before.

One of the best reactions I can imagine someone having to

this book, or any single section of this book would be, "Huh, I never thought of that." I would love for these words to propel that simple switch that opens your world to so many new possibilities.

On the other hand, it's important to not put so much value in someone else's advice that we ignore our own inner voice. Just as much as I want to show you a new perspective, spark a new idea, or motivate you to do that thing you've been thinking about for years, I want you to allow yourself to listen only to the things that resonate with you...whether they excite you, scare you, make you laugh, make you think, or all of the above. But if they do nothing for you, that's totally ok! Not everything is for everyone.

So, think of this book as a friend who's sitting down next to you, listening to you talk, and sharing some stories to give you a different perspective. No prescriptions, no directions, no requirements, and definitely no pressure. Let this book be a buddy you can visit whenever you want, that you can say goodbye to and know will be there when you come back. That would make me really happy.

If you're going through something specific and looking for a little solace or inspiration or a different perspective, check out the table of contents and see if I've already written about it. If you're just looking for some random inspiration, flip to any darn page of the book you want and see if something clicks. I don't pretend to have all the answers, and some of the answers that worked for me might not work for you. Although I maintain that snuggling with a puppy is probably one of the top five happy-makers in the world, especially my little Charley (and if you disagree I will fight you on this). Even if you just want to flip through the book and look at the gorgeous illustrations, I completely support you in that choice.

LET THIS BOOK BE A BUDDY YOU CAN VISIT WHENEVER YOU WANT, THAT YOU CAN SAY GOODBYE TO AND KNOW WILL BE THERE WHEN YOU COME BACK.

This book is about living a big, beautiful, wild, exciting, *fun* life full of all kinds of experiences. And that means: your life, your rules. The only thing I really, really hope you do is enjoy yourself while reading this.

Thanks for letting me go on this journey with you. Because I am Fun Size, and so are YOU.

HELLLOOOOOOOOOOOO!

THE STRUGGLE IS REAL (SERIOUSLY)

Even though the above words are often sarcastically used these days to describe something ironically unimportant, the truth is for many of us, the struggle *is* real. Whether we are in dire financial straits, in a painful relationship we don't know how to extricate ourselves from, dealing with a major health issue, or facing any number of genuinely difficult circumstances, the struggle we may find ourselves in can be wildly overwhelming. So much so that the instinct, understandably, may be to say (to me or others):

"You don't understand. You don't have the same problems I do."

"Yeah, but my issues are *real* problems and I need a *real* solution."

"It's easy for you to say."

Having said the above, or variations on the theme, many times in my life when I *did* find myself in dire straits, I get it. I truly do. I've been $90K in debt with no work in sight. I've been heartbroken on my knees, unsure the pain and tears would ever stop, wondering how I would get through the next five minutes, let alone the next day, week, month, or year. I've been deeply depressed, lost, broke, unemployed. And as hard as it is to admit, there were days in my past when I woke up and wished I hadn't.

What I'm going to say here is not an easy thing to say. In fact, it may be one of the hardest, and you may scoff or roll your eyes at me but *please* believe I say this from knowing what rock bottom feels like: When things in your life—real world problems—are at the absolute worst, that's when it's most vital to take even the tiniest step toward the light and trust that amazing things are possible.

I'm talking about *one* step closer to feeling better, not going from severe depression to unimaginable joy; that's a ridiculous leap for anyone to expect of themselves. I'm here to help you succeed, not set unrealistic expectations and hate yourself for not meeting them (hi, welcome to half my life). Just one thought better, one moment lighter, turning your ship one tenth of one degree off the path you've been on can lead to a completely different life; it can steer the Titanic out of the path of the iceberg and on toward warmer climes.

> **WHEN THINGS IN YOUR LIFE - REAL WORLD PROBLEMS - ARE AT THE ABSOLUTE WORST, THAT'S WHEN IT'S MOST VITAL TO TAKE EVEN THE TINIEST STEP TOWARD THE LIGHT AND TRUST THAT AMAZING THINGS ARE POSSIBLE.**

Some of the tools I mention or self-reflections I write about in the upcoming pages may feel as if they come from a place of privilege, of having the luxury of time and freedom and resources to do so much inner work. And you know what? To an extent, you're right. I chose a career in which my very livelihood is dependent on my exploration of the inner workings of the human mind, of emotions, of what makes us tick. That is *such* a privilege.

But that doesn't mean that any of what I'm sharing in the pages was easy for me to learn or to put into practice, especially when I was broke and/or broken, so deep in depression that I couldn't find the strength or knowledge to fight my way out, so consumed with self-loathing that I didn't believe I was even *worth* fighting for. Those times are precisely the reason I'm asking you to take my hand, to let me be here with you in this dark cave. I don't use humor to diminish the importance of what you're going through, or what any of us are going through; I use it to remind us we can lighten that load just by changing even one little thing. A small laugh can make a huge difference.

I am on a mission to make sure as many people as possible don't go through what I did to learn these lessons, or at the very least, know they are not alone while they do. I know that, thanks to my incredibly tumultuous journey within myself combined with my career choice, I have a unique ability to experience emotions others don't have the freedom, safe space, or ability to experience.

This is ultimately why I picked acting as my weapon of choice to pursue this mission, this purpose. My job, as I see it, is to take the hand of everyone in the audience and say, "I've got you. For the time we are together, I'm going to walk you through this story, this experience. I'll do the heavy lifting, experience the high highs and the low lows.

You can feel them with me and through me, safely from your seat. And at the end of our time together, you'll be able to return to your life just as it was when we met, all the pieces intact, but with a little more knowledge because you went on this ride with me. And my hope is that you feel fuller for it." And now, I'm extending that form of connection to writing. Hopefully through experiencing some of my challenges with me, safely wherever you are, you'll be able to benefit a little from someone else's journey. Or again, at least know you're not alone.

> **I DON'T USE HUMOR TO DIMINISH THE IMPORTANCE OF WHAT YOU'RE GOING THROUGH, OR WHAT ANY OF US ARE GOING THROUGH; I USE IT TO REMIND US WE CAN LIGHTEN THAT LOAD JUST BY CHANGING EVEN ONE LITTLE THING. A SMALL LAUGH CAN MAKE A HUGE DIFFERENCE.**

Trust me, no matter where you are—in your life, career, love life, or on the planet—being Fun Size isn't impossible; *you already are*. And whether you have $10 million or $10, whether you are married to the love of your life and are dancing on Cloud Nine or you've just had yet another heartbreak, whether you are living the life of your dreams or you can't even see your way out of the dark, you are *so worthy* of a big, beautiful, Fun Size life. It is already around you and inside you. So come with me for now…I've got you.

THE FUN SIZE HERO'S JOURNEY

HOW WE THINK IT WILL GO:

WHAT IT FEELS LIKE WHEN WE'RE IN IT:

WHAT IT LOOKS LIKE LOOKING BACK AT THE END:

I've seen so many maps of the creative process and of the life process, some of them humorous, some of them instructive, but the fact is, I've never seen one that quite matched the exact path *I've* been on. While time might be a linear concept (at least for now...who knows what quantum physicists will discover in the next 5, 10, 50, 100 years), our life journeys are not. And while I can definitely look back on certain events that make perfect sense in retrospect, there have been so many ups and downs and diagonals and loop-de-loops in my life so far—and I'm not even halfway done!—that I know better than to try to diagram what the journey "should" look like.

Still, I'm going to attempt to divide this book into three parts of the journey because I do think that these phases have repeated each other to varying degrees and depths throughout my life, and the more times I go through any of them, the more I am heartened by the fact that I know that none of them are permanent. Whether it is the excitement (or panic) and promise of a new beginning, the challenge of an inner battle or difficult circumstances, or the relief of a goal hard won (and the odd comedown that sometimes follows), each of these stages of the journey has its own joys and sorrows, its own challenges and triumphs. In each of the three parts, I'll share a little of what I've learned (or what I know I've yet to learn) over the times I've been through them again and again.

Part 1

In the Beginning

"The beginning is always today."
-Mary Shelley

Anjali Bhimani

PANIC! AT THE ~~DISCO~~ STARTING LINE

So many things can hold us back from the big, beautiful, Fun Size life we imagine for ourselves. Some practical or physical limitations—like money, time, trauma, mental or physical health. But then there's that pesky and incredibly unhelpful feeling that keeps us from even getting to the starting line, that feeling of being too behind for it to be worth even starting.

I remember the first time I felt so behind on learning something that I didn't even think it was worth starting. All my peers in the same discipline were so far ahead of me; there was no way I was going to catch up. Everyone I had read about or heard about, all these heroes of mine in this discipline had started much younger than I already was, not to mention their natural given talent for this art. There was no way I could just start it now and have any success or even any joy. The learning curve was obviously steep, and in order for me to get good enough to really feel proud of myself (which at that time meant catching up to and surpassing the people around me), I would have to put in so many hours of blood, sweat, and many, many tears that it just made more sense not to start at all.

The discipline? Dance.

My age? 11 years old. ELEVEN.

So yeah, I'm familiar with that demon voice in our heads

that tells us it's too late. He's been barking at me since grade school. And not only is he wrong, he's a TOTAL DICK.

Like me, I'm guessing you've heard this voice a time or two trying to convince you it's too late to learn a new skill, choose a new career, find love, heal from heartbreak, heal from *anything*. And then there are the deeper, more insidious and ineffable things that pesky demon says it's too late for. Too late to forgive or be forgiven, too late to change old habits that have hurt you for years, too late to repair a wounded relationship...the list goes on and on.

It's easy to listen to that voice that says it's too late, urges us not to even try. What's *not* easy is dealing with the damage that mindset can do to us when a year, five years, ten years down the line, we realize we probably *could* have started those piano lessons, written that book, had that clearing conversation with a family member that might have changed our relationship for the better. It can be devastating to look back and realize that baby steps along the way would have led us somewhere different, maybe even somewhere better, than where we are now.

Well, I'm here to tell you it's never too late to start to care for yourself, to love more and hurt less, to laugh more and enjoy the time you have left with yourself or others, to try out those singing lessons, art courses, cooking classes, (whatever!) just to see if you really do love it as much as you thought you would. The thing that I think really keeps us from doing it is believing that if we don't meet a certain expectation or some lofty goal we've set for ourselves (or has been set for us by someone else), it will all be useless.

You know what I've *never* heard someone say?

"Man, I wish my mom had never made me take piano lessons as a kid. It's awful having a deeper appreciation of music."

"It really sucks that I spent all that time learning how to speak Japanese. I wish I didn't know how to connect deeply with people of another culture in their own native language."

"I wish I hadn't started treating myself better. I miss feeling like crap."

"I wish I'd never forgiven that person who wronged me. That jealousy and anger would have done so much good for me and my well-being over the last few years."

But I *have* heard plenty of people say, "I really wish I had learned/tried/done [insert their dream left in the past here]." Including myself.

It doesn't matter what happened before. It doesn't matter what you *haven't* done. All that matters is what you want to do today and all the days to come. In my experience, all that not starting does is keep you from the joy of new experiences, of growth, of definitively knowing, "Oh hey, I actually *don't* like doing this. Cool. Lemme not do it then."

IT DOESN'T MATTER WHAT YOU HAVEN'T DONE. ALL THAT MATTERS IS WHAT YOU WANT TO DO TODAY AND ALL THE DAYS TO COME.

Incidentally, I didn't start taking dance classes until I was 15 years old. At 22, I was dancing a solo at the Kennedy Center. At 30, I was dancing in a blockbuster musical on Broadway. Turned out it wasn't too late to start. And you better believe I'm planning to enjoy dancing for years to come.

And that wasn't the only time I started something late in the game, despite knowing it was "late." I started auditioning for voiceovers in 2014. I was 40. I married the love of my life at 43. At 90, I hope to be learning a new language because I love them so much. I will suck at it at first, and I will love the joy of accomplishment as I go, because it's never too late to enjoy the process of learning or becoming something new, *n'est-ce pas?*

CHARLEY LESSON #1: MAMA, CHILL.

It was the first day of having this mind-blowingly adorable, sweet, snuggly ball of fur in my home, and he was scampering and sniffing and snuggling his way all over the house. Meanwhile, I was having a full-blown, anxiety-ridden melt-down:

What am I DOING? I don't know how to raise a DOG! I mean, I've read 10 books in the last week and I puppy-proofed every inch of this apartment, I spent half my monthly food budget on special lidded trash cans that he can't get into, and I've sprayed all the cords and corners of wooden furniture with bitter apple so he won't chew them. I've made sure all the foods he can't eat—which I have also kept on a laminated list prominently displayed in the kitchen—are far out of his doggie reach, but still, I'm just so scared I'm gonna do this wrong and something is going to happen to this perfect little guy.

Somewhere in the middle of that meltdown, I looked down at Charley's tiny, precious face peering up at me from under my desk, and it was as if he was beaming words into my brain: "Mama, chill. I have toys. I have food. And you're gonna take me out to pee, right? I'm good. I just need more snuggles. Like *lots* of snuggles."

To this day, I will catch Charley looking at me with that "Mama, chill" look, and when I am a little *too* stubborn in my worry, he'll look at me, huff, sigh, turn around, and walk out the door. If he could shake his head and roll his eyes, he probably would.

So, a little lesson from C-Dawg: When you're getting so wound up that you can't think straight, remember the basics. Roof over your head, food in your belly, snuggles in your life. (You're welcome to take yourself for a walk, too, but the outdoor peeing is probably best left to Charley and his puppy brethren).

CHOOSE YOUR OWN NEW YEAR (AS MANY TIMES AS YOU WANT)!

Every year around December 31, thanks to our dependence on the good ol' Gregorian calendar, there seems to be a mad rush in the lives of millions of self-actualizing people to choose a resolution, set intentions, clear the decks, make a plan, set goals, get ready to hit the ground running—you name it.

But we know how the story goes: The goals get set, the resolutions made, the plans hashed out, and then somehow come January 31 (or January 3), we are filled with shame and regret because we've already lost sight of them. Whether life got in the way or we forgot our "why," whether our get-up-and-go got up and went, or we just couldn't pull it off in time, we feel disappointed in ourselves and think that somehow we've failed. Oh well. There's always next year.

No. No, no, no, no, no! You don't need December 31 or January 1 or any other specific date on the calendar to give you the freedom to restart, renew, re-commit, or review anything in your life. It's a cliché but it's true: Today is the first day of the rest of your life. It's a new day. It's a *perfect* time to start again.

And if you need a holiday on the calendar to help motivate you to do it, trust me, just a tiny bit of Googling and you'll find a National SOMETHING Day for every freakin' day of the year.

"Today? It's National Pralines Day! This is a *perfect* day for me to restart that eating plan and cut out sugar. And when I make it through the month, my one sugary treat will be—ta DA!—PRALINES!"

"Oh yeah, it's National Parchment Day today, so I thought it was a perfect time for me to restart that writing project I started at the beginning of the year. I'm gonna handwrite a little bit of it in honor of the day."

"It's National Puppy Day!" Wait, every day really should be National Puppy Day…because puppies…

IT'S A CLICHÉ BUT IT'S TRUE: TODAY IS THE FIRST DAY OF THE REST OF YOUR LIFE. IT'S A NEW DAY. IT'S A PERFECT TIME TO START AGAIN.

I choose dates to start things based on the story I want to be true at the finish line. A few New Years back, I wanted to make a massive shift in my health practices, not an uncommon goal for people to take on at the beginning of the year. But, as often happens, life got in the way and it didn't quite stick. Then, months later, I started again on my birthday but, nope, still not the right time.

Then came my anniversary. I decided it was an auspicious date to start because a huge part of the reason I wanted to change my ways was because of something my husband had once said: "Please take care of yourself. I need you to be around a really long time." (Cue the waterworks.)

My health—no longer worrying about my weight and size, just being healthy—would be a wonderful gift to him. Whatever size I am, Rick wants me to be healthy, having fun, and feeling good—ya know, Fun Size. And that time, it stuck!

Instead of letting the day of the week tell me when to start, I'll *find* a reason that today is the right day. "Oh, starting on Friday is perfect because I was born on a Friday (cue Gandalf-style epic wizard voice):

AND TODAY I SHALL BE REBOOOORRRRRRNNNN."

The point is, don't let the calendar diminish your enthusiasm for doing the things you want or need to do. After all, time is a construct, just something we humans created to make sense of the world and organize what is happening in it. So your New Year could start at 3:48 p.m. on June 23. It really doesn't matter. What matters is YOU—coming at your desires and dreams and goals renewed, refreshed, and ready to go.

Part 1: In The Beginning

Jeannie Bolet
Voice Actress (Overwatch), Screenwriter, Jewelry Maker, Fellow Dog Mom
www.iamfunsize.com/jeanniebolet

"There's that saying: 'You made your bed; you better sleep in it.' Someone said it to me when I was feeling down and stuck with the decisions I'd made. But one of the first friends that I met in L.A., Sarju Patel, I remember him saying, 'Well, you can tell them that you will make your bed again, and you can keep making it and making it until it feels like it's right for you.' It was such a great reminder that we aren't stuck but actually at the intersection of choice, and that we can all be agents of change in our own life."

Ready! Set! Wait....Where Am I Going Again?

For most of my life, I was so busy do-do-doing things, that I didn't take the time to figure out which of the things I wanted to keep doing and which of the things I could let go. I knew I wanted to be a successful actress, but there were so many great ways to do that, I couldn't set my heart on one, and I didn't want to! I knew I wanted to make more money, but I wasn't sure how I wanted to do it. I knew I wanted to find a beautiful, loving relationship, but everything I read in magazines or the advice I was being given felt somehow just not *me*. Everything I read about setting goals and intentions was smacking me in the face with mandates like, "You have to be specific about what you want, down to the last detail," or "Make sure you focus all your energy on this one goal or you'll never achieve it."

The idea of being this specific gave me anxiety. I didn't want to have to choose, didn't want to exclude the possibility of something else more exciting, rewarding, fulfilling, or magical down the line. I would sit there spinning about all the things I wanted to do or have or be, never really able to settle on one. So I wouldn't. I would just give up on the goal setting and let myself be blown through life like a leaf on the wind.

Eventually, I stumbled upon a more Fun Size way of setting goals, of choosing the things I wanted to pursue in my life.

Instead of following the script, instead of specifically naming a goal of working with a certain director or getting a certain amount of money in the bank, I began working with my actress brain and my heart on a different approach, one that felt right for me. I began focusing less on the tangible goal and more on how that goal would make me *feel*. (I know what you're thinking: "Wow, Anj, you weren't kidding when you said you were a little woo-woo." But stay with me. This may be the turn of the kaleidoscope you've been missing.)

When I wanted to find a partner, I didn't want to exclude him because of any external descriptors. I didn't know what I wanted him to look like, but I definitely knew how I wanted to *feel* in that relationship. I didn't know the exact acting job I wanted, and I didn't want to exclude anything I couldn't imagine at the moment, but I knew how I wanted to *feel* on set with my cast working with a dream director.

Imagining these feelings, cultivating them inside me, feeling them deeply and fully even without knowing the specifics of the circumstances that would cause those feelings, would fill me with so much light and life and energy that choosing the next right action would just sort of come to me. I could tell who I did and didn't want to spend time with based on whether it felt the way I had imagined it feeling. I knew what jobs I would take or not take based on the gut instinct of how it would feel. Using my feelings as a guidepost, I was better able to hone down specifics along the way and adjust my goals day by day if needed. I began to learn what did and didn't make me feel the way I wanted to feel.

Before I met my husband, I really didn't know what the relationship I wanted to be in would look like. If I'm being honest, I think several years of trying to force myself to be happy in relationships that weren't right had me not trusting my "picker," not trusting the things I thought I wanted in a partner.

And so, when I was working through my last breakup and achieving what I lovingly refer to as "head-from-ass extraction," I found myself imagining scenes—scenes from a life I had no idea how I would get, but it felt good. I imagined cutting flowers at a kitchen island and feeling strong arms wrap around me from behind, a sweet face nuzzling into my neck while a little dog ran in from the kitchen door. I sank into the warmth of that simple moment, that simple dream, so frequently. And while the island hasn't shown up yet (although I do love our kitchen all the same), the most important pieces of that moment—the little dog, the strong arms, the sweet face—did.

I'm not saying I somehow cast some witchery-doo with my dream, but leaning into how I wanted to feel did prepare me for when that feeling came. What's even more fun is when you finally get to that place you aspired to after imagining and living in the feeling for so long, the joy of succeeding comes with a wave of recognition—a feeling that says, "I know this place. This feels right to me."

So ask yourself: how do you want to feel in a relationship? In your body? With your family? In your career? How do you want to feel in your home? In relationship with yourself? In your spiritual or religious practice? Or just: how do you want to feel when you wake up in the morning or go to bed at night? Answering these questions (whether in your head or with an actual old school pen and paper) might just make your path clearer.

For example, here's something I wrote when I wasn't feeling particularly great about my physical wellness. I knew it was easy for me to focus on outward appearance (just like everyone else in the world), but what I was really going for was how I wanted to feel in my body. (I like to write as if it already *is* rather than using "I want" language; it keeps me from feeling like I don't have it yet.)

I am energized and ready to face the day each morning. My body may take a little time to wake up, but it's not creaky or achy or in pain, just needs a little morning love—maybe a good stretch or a walk with Charley. I have loads of energy to face everything I have to do during the day. I don't have to depend on coffee (even though I still drink it because I love it, thank you very much) or anything else to keep me going. I am strong enough to do everything I need to do throughout my day. I feel proud of how I walk through the world. I'm all set to jump into that action role I've been waiting to start shooting. I know I'm going to nail it and have fun the whole time I'm on set.

So what makes this different than the typical old school affirmations we've all heard or read about? The tangible, practical next step. After I write that out, I'll imagine one moment—in this case, maybe it's doing a bunch of pull-ups on set. (I suck at pull-ups right now thanks to a weak shoulder, so being able to do them, especially for the work I love, would make me feel like a million dollars.) That feeling of accomplishment and pride and power? *That's* as much a part of my goal as those sweet, sweet reps. So what can I do in *this* moment to take a step closer to *that* moment? Assisted or reverse pull-ups. Even just one here and one there. I'm gonna need to practice them daily in order to get to that feeling. It could happen tomorrow. It could happen a year from now. There's no telling, so I better get right on it.

(Be right back…running to the pull-up bar in the bedroom and taking down the clothes that are hanging on it so I can practice…even just one pull up. Right. Freakin'. Now.)

PART 1: IN THE BEGINNING

ARE YOU RUNNING FROM SOMETHING OR RUNNING TO SOMETHING?

A little bit of a sad story here, but one that unfortunately is all too common among young women (and men) in our society. When I first started working out in my teens (when I was trying to make up for my seemingly chronic unathleticism), it was mostly a process of beating the crap out of myself on the inside for what I saw on the outside. Whether it was from reading too many beauty magazines or just the general result of living in a very outwardly focused culture, I had a terrible body image and felt that if I didn't stay in perfect shape, I would be fundamentally unlovable.

I would work out for hours every day just to have enough peace of mind to allow myself to eat. (Never mind the fact that we have to eat to live, and that food is one of the greatest joys in life.) When I did work out, I would feel a tiny bit of relief that I had earned my worthiness for the day. And when I didn't work out, I would feel guilty about every morsel I put in my mouth. I basically lived in constant fear of being unloved, unworthy, uncastable as an actress, you name it, just to keep myself doing a simple thing that was good for me. And ultimately, because of that mentality, it wasn't good for me.

When I look back on those years, it blows my mind how much I tried to motivate myself by terrifying myself. Yeah, fear can be an excellent motivator...for a while. The only problem with using it as the *sole* motivator is that you create a constant environment of worry and anxiety that doesn't allow you to enjoy the successes or the wins. I may have been physically healthy, but my mindset was so, so wrong that my body never *felt* good, not from the inside.

There came a point where I was so burnt out from my own self-flagellation and physical exhaustion that I simply had to give up; the energy I was spending—mental, emotional, physical, spiritual—was so great that I had completely depleted myself and fallen into a depression of my own making.

In later years, I learned to give exercise over to my favorite activities: dancing, hiking, playing with Charley. And amazingly enough, when I leaned into the joy, the relishing, the positive outcomes of doing these activities, my body settled into a comfort and a health that I had never known during all those years I was berating myself so hard.

The very same thing happened with my grades. As an ambitious, straight-A student, I worked diligently, did all my homework, studied hard for tests, and got great grades. But in my mind it was always, "Okay. I got an A this time, but what about the next time?" It was always, "What if I don't get an A and I'm a huge failure?" (I'm not sure if I am comforted or disturbed by the knowledge that I am definitely not the only human who considered B+ to be a failing grade.) I was constantly running away from failure rather than leaning into success. I never gave myself the pride or the comfort or the self-satisfaction of a job well done. I just focused on what I was running from.

As I moved into my college years and began to study courses that were specific to my own personal passion, I had a wonderful conversation with my acting teacher at the time, Mary Poole. Mary was, and is, a force of nature. She taught us to cultivate a zest for life and engage with all experiences this world had to offer. Those lessons are still with me today. She also taught us exercises for allowing ourselves to be vulnerable on stage and taking power from that.

> **I WAS CONSTANTLY RUNNING AWAY FROM FAILURE RATHER THAN LEANING INTO SUCCESS. I NEVER GAVE MYSELF THE PRIDE OR THE COMFORT OR THE SELF-SATISFACTION OF A JOB WELL DONE.**

But in this instance, I had gone up to her office because that quarter, I can't even remember what it was we were studying specifically, she had given me an A- instead of an A in acting. I was flabbergasted. How could I have gotten an A-? What was wrong with me? What did I do wrong? How did I fail so hard? How did I miss the mark? When I went to her office to ask her those questions, she just said very calmly, "You just didn't get this one quite as well as you've gotten the rest. It's no big deal." In her eyes, it was just an assessment, not a moral judgment. But to me, it was a sign of my failure as a human being. Mary proceeded to say, "I think you need to fail more." I didn't understand what she meant at the time, but now it's a lot clearer.

As you're on the path, running *toward* success, you are going to make mistakes. You are going to slip off the path. You are going to fail. And that's totally okay because you are still running *toward* something. When you fail and you don't die, you prove to yourself that failure won't kill you. You find the courage to keep chasing success.

When I'm struggling with a task or a goal, when I'm uninspired to do basic things that I know are important to me—my health, my career, my family—when I'm struggling with motivation and inspiration, I'll take a moment to ask: Am I running *from* something or running *to* something? Am I running from fear of failure, fear of being judged, fear of unworthiness? Or am I running to something beautiful? Where is my "why" coming from? Is it coming from me intrinsically or is it coming from some extrinsic factor? Am I judging my worth as an actor by whether or not someone else hires me for a job, or am I judging it by how I actually feel about my own work and the joy it gives me and the joy it gives other people?

Sure, running from things can be an effective motivator. Fear will give you that sudden rush of energy. But it is not always sustainable. It will eventually run you down, discourage you so much that you stop trying altogether. What *is* sustainable is looking forward instead of backward, looking toward the things you want to create in the world, running toward happiness, toward self-satisfaction, toward making your loved ones feel loved and content, toward a big, beautiful, Fun Size life. Now *that* you can sustain for all the days to come.

Part 1: In The Beginning

Discipline Is Deciding

On our first girls' night out, I mentioned a new workout routine I had been diligently following to my friend, Poorna Jagannathan, someone I admire wildly for her grace, beauty, talent, intelligence, humor…I mean I could go on for days about her. When I look at what she has accomplished in her life, I am in complete and utter awe. So when she said to me, "Wow, you're so disciplined," after I picked my jaw up off the floor, given how undisciplined I thought I was, I found myself saying, "I'm not disciplined, I just…decided," to which she replied, simply, "That's discipline."

Whoa. The wisdom in what she had just said hit me like I'd been smacked by one of those 20-pound dumbbells I'd recently gotten used to hefting around. I could have saved myself *years* of self-flagellation and misery had I realized that simple truth on my own:

I don't need to "find" discipline, I just need to decide.

Now, stick with me here because, yes, discipline is a real thing, but frankly, I think the concept of it has been a little warped for many of us. We've imagined it as something we have or don't have, and that there is a moral judgment to be placed on those who don't miraculously have it in spades, rather than as something that is the product of cultivation and making certain decisions with regularity.

I have never, ever, *ever* thought of myself as a disciplined person. Left to my own devices, I will sit on a couch scrolling through dog videos, frequent traveler/credit card points program blogs, and real estate listings (hey, those are my happy places, don't judge), and suddenly find myself frustrated that I didn't get any work done. If I don't actually force myself to get up at a certain hour to get things done by thinking of something important and enjoyable (that second part is *clutch)* I have to do, I will happily sleep in for hours, especially since we have somehow cracked the code on having the most comfortable bed and sheets and comforter in all humanity (and once Charley snuggles in next to me, forget it, I'm done for). I have been known to whine about having to walk upstairs because I forgot something, let alone about having to go to the gym or do anything that is remotely difficult. I like life *easy*.

The tricky part is, I also have dreams and aspirations of experiencing things that require a certain degree of actual effort placed. So that lovely day of sitting on the couch scrolling through Dogstagram really does have to wait.

Maddeningly, I have also spent God knows how much time in my life judging myself for being lazy instead of focusing on the fact that the only reason I wasn't feeling inspired to do something was that I hadn't given myself enough reason, enough deep motivation, to *decide* that change mattered.

Now, am I saying that change is easy? Of course not. But it can be simple. I do think that we use the excuse of, "I'm just not disciplined," to let ourselves off the hook *and* beat ourselves up at the same time. The truth is, we just haven't made the decision to *do* something to create the result we want.

I think so much of what we think is a lack of discipline is just us not making a choice. Again, if left to my own devices, if I am not intentional about where I want to put my focus on any given day, just like many other people, I will find myself wiling away the time doing any number of things that are ultimately unsatisfying because I didn't really make the choice to focus on them. I have been the QUEEN of unintentional busyness so many times in my life (even recently, as I have been needing to make many decisions to be able to focus on writing over just "keeping busy").

There is even a certain discipline to intentionally taking the time to have fun doing something. Because you have *decided* you are going to spend this time focusing on friends or entertainment or something that gives you joy, you've exercised those discipline muscles. The amount of focus and intention that I and my friends put into our tabletop role-playing games is a perfect example of how to take your fun seriously, as evidenced by some of the shows we've played them on, such as *We're Alive:Frontier, Undeadwood,* or *Exandria Unlimited.* The game ends up being incredibly satisfying because of the focus and commitment to the activity.

I imagine people who play competitive sports for fun feel the same way, and I know that dancers understand the feeling. The rush of how hard you push during a dance number when you're feeling the music, feeling the thrill of moving your body in challenging but beautiful ways. I remember doing *The Jungle Book* at the Goodman Theatre in 2013, and during the final moments of the act one finale, I did a series of jump squats for so long that every night I would tell myself, *Well, if I die of a heart attack tonight, this will be a hell of a way to go, but I'm NOT... STOPPING... THESE... JUMPS.*

Deciding. Focusing. Intending.

I have spent so much more energy trying to decide if I was going to work out on any given day—negotiating with myself whether it was worth it that day because, oh, I'm so tired or I have so much to do—than I have *actually working out*. But my proverbial "aha" moment came on a recent birthday when I was grumbling about my health to someone I adore (but who shall remain nameless because they would feel just awful, and really, I should be thanking them profusely for this comment) who said, "Welcome to middle age, darling." I responded, "Yeah, but I mean, Rick is older than me, and he says he feels better than ever," to which sweet relative replied, "But these are our genes. Auntie paunch."

At that very moment, I decided, "Oh, hell no. I'm going to do whatever I have to do to overcome this (evidently genetic) middle-aged thing." Not long after, I found a gym and trainer (God bless you, Eddie Baruta) who changed my life in two days. That's not an exaggeration. TWO days. Because at the end of the second workout, my mood was so drastically shifted that I knew my body was going to follow. I found so much relief and reclaimed energy in giving up the inner argument between working out or not...energy I had been spending at war with myself on the inside, depleting myself more than the actual act of change would.

And then I was angry at myself. I had spent years and years hating my body and complaining about it when all I had to do was *decide*. Hell, I'd spent 10 years lamenting the loss of my "dancer butt" and it only took about 12 weeks to get it back. And while the support of brilliant, patient, and encouraging Eddie, the intense eating plan, and lifting more weights than I had in my entire life all helped, none of that would have mattered if I hadn't first *decided it* was costing me more energy and happiness to not take action than it was to actually do the surprisingly short and effective workouts I'd been avoiding. For that period of time, it wasn't some magical quality of discipline that got me to work out. But it *was* deciding I didn't want to feel shitty about myself and my choices anymore.

But discipline isn't just about deciding *to* do something; it also takes discipline to decide *not* to do something, to make the decision that maybe you need to focus your attention and energy toward something else, or that you know your limitations and it might not be the best time to take on something massive. Recently I have found myself not thinking big picture when making decisions, not fully considering my priorities and the finite amount of time and energy I have. As a result, I've not been disciplined enough to say no when I need to.

The frustrating part is, I will be genuinely overworked or overwhelmed by too much going on, but I will chalk that up to—you guessed it—"I don't have enough discipline." This then turns into a series of negative comments in my head and beating myself up for letting myself down. The simpler solution would be saying, *Anj. Make a decision. If you do this, you will have to give up something else. Which matters more in the moment?* and then living into the decision I make, knowing that that it was *my choice*.

I've also learned when I get off track it's usually because I've shifted the priorities in my mind. Note for both of us: Your priorities will change. THIS IS NORMAL. You didn't just lose your discipline, never to find it again. You aren't a failure as a human for being in a different phase of your journey. You...WE...just changed our priorities. The trick is making sure the shift in priorities is intentional...or at least a shift you want to be making. Not a gradual slide into, "Oh huh, I haven't been paying much attention. I think I've been scrolling Instagram and binging Netflix for six weeks straight and I don't even remember what I watched."

Right now, I have had to accept that I don't have the energy to devote to hard-core workouts or eating plans because I'm happily and intentionally putting all my best energy into this love bomb of a book. I've decided that rather than set a goal for myself to be as fit as Brie Larson in her training for Captain Marvel, I'm going to be a different kind of superhero and flex my creative muscles to get this love letter out in the world (although you better believe if Marvel calls, this book is gonna have to wait). I still have a goal of being active and feeling good in my body while I write, but I can't put 100% of my energy into every goal I have.*

---

*Incidentally, Eddie was also instrumental in my realization of the importance of this in recent months. His reminders to have realistic expectations of my own levels of energy and focus, and not to beat myself up for prioritizing what I needed, were a godsend, just like his expertise in the gym was when we worked together. I owe so much learning to him.

We have to prioritize. We have to decide where to direct our focus. We have to decide to do whatever it takes to make our priorities happen, whatever they are—family, love, fitness, career, whatever. And we have to decide not to let ourselves be thrown off track. We have to *just keep deciding*. That's a recipe for some Fun Size living right there. Because, let's be honest, it's a lot more fun to *decide* than to "have discipline." Discipline sounds like a chore. Deciding means it's my *choice*. And as I mentioned at the beginning of this book, my stubbornness will kick in if I feel like I'm doing something that isn't my own decision. Discipline is saying, "I have to"; deciding is saying, "I get to." And "get to" sounds way more fun to me.

LET'S BE HONEST, IT'S A LOT MORE FUN TO DECIDE THAN TO 'HAVE DISCIPLINE.' DISCIPLINE SOUNDS LIKE A CHORE. DECIDING MEANS IT'S MY CHOICE.

P.S. Brie, if you're reading this, call me. I do wanna compare gym notes with you for when this 114-year-old becomes the hottest GILF superhero ever.

IT'S JUST DO IT, NOT JUST SHARE IT

So, confession time: I've been very guilty in the past of talking about my great big plans for things and then...well...not following through. That super cool script idea, that idea for a podcast, that idea for a TikTok account or invention or t-shirt, so many great ideas have come out of my mouth only to stop right there. Just a bunch of words sent out into the world in exchange for a little bit of support or positive response, and then, pfft! They fizzle out like a dud firecracker on the 4th of July.

Thanks to social media, there's a bit of pressure these days to tell the world everything you're working on. Or thinking of working on. Or thinking of thinking of working on. (You get the point.) The onslaught of "Challenges" that came out during the COVID-19 pandemic made it feel like everything had to be posted online to be a valid accomplishment. The "21-Day This" or the "30-Day That" or the "3-Times-a-Day Whatever" had me wanting to spend 30 days punching someone in the neck. It's great to have an accountability partner or group in your life to help you stay on track, but there is an interesting phenomenon that can happen when you share your plans with others before you actually start them.

There is a widely referenced study[1] that suggests sharing our goals sometimes gives us enough of the feeling of having accomplished them to actually *deter* us from doing the work to get there. The researchers found that the social recognition we get can feel as good to us as having accomplished our goals. A post about how you're going to apply to law school can (and should) invite a heap of comments like, "You go, girl!" "That's great!" "You've got this," even before you've cracked open an LSAT study guide. But it may also be just enough affirmation to fill the need so you let those applications sit on your computer desktop for another month or two.

When I came across that study, it was like a personal affront. *Shit. I used to do this all the time. (Pause) Okay, who am I kidding, I STILL do this.* In fact (and it's hard to admit this), this book is a great example. I would *talk* about the book I wanted to write. I would get tons of praise for the idea, for my resourcefulness, for my creativity. But when it came down to actually writing? I was very happy just being praised for my idea. It felt good to be lauded for my brilliance without actually having to do any heavy lifting.

RESEARCHERS FOUND THAT THE SOCIAL RECOGNITION WE GET CAN FEEL AS GOOD TO US AS HAVING ACCOMPLISHED OUR GOALS.

What finally got me to do it? Starting before I told anyone around me what I was doing. Starting it for *me* because I wanted to do some good in the world in a new way. I eventually let some people know I was working on it, mostly so they understood why I was cancelling so many things or turning down their invitations, but also to keep me accountable. I needed a select few people in my life who wouldn't let me get away with saying I was doing it but not actually doing it.

Did I post online at the beginning of my journey? HELL no. I wanted to make sure I did something before I let myself have the satisfaction of accomplishing the thing. And sure enough, when I was well on my way and the positive reinforcement of seeing my progress was keeping me going, *then* I started to share my journey. But the motivation came from me; the support of others just spurred me onward.

Added bonus? You don't get anyone else's negative or stuck energy on you while you're busy making something happen for yourself. Unfortunately, no matter how well-intentioned, some people can't help but let their own baggage inform how they respond to others making big changes in their lives. You're on a mission; don't let anyone else being on their own path keep you from staying the course on yours.

As for all those big plans you have in your head that you haven't started yet but really want to? Get them on the calendar—*your* calendar—and have that conversation with *yourself* about how cool it will be to do it. Don't allow yourself to share the idea (except maybe with a few dear confidantes or potential collaborators) until you know full well you can commit to the decision to get it done. And then, it's off to the proverbial races.

In short, we all know the slogan. It's just *do* it, not just *share* it. So, get cracking on your goal for *you*. Maybe choose a select group of people who won't let you let *yourself* down. Then, let the rest of the world be amazed when you share the magic you've already made.

JUST BECAUSE YOU CAN HAVE IT ALL DOESN'T MEAN YOU HAVE TO

I have two memories from my teen years that showed me the power of being free to focus. The first came from my beloved brother, Anish, who I don't have words enough to tell you about in this whole book. Throughout my life he has been an inspiration, a protector, a guide, a fervent supporter, a partner-in-crime, a playmate, and a best friend. But he laid this moment of incredible wisdom on me in junior high when I was doing everything I could to follow in his footsteps. I wanted to be him so badly, to do what he did, to love what he loved, to have all the same skills and talents—and he saw it.

One day, with great love, he said to me, "Listen, there are things in the world that you love and that you are great at that I will never love or be good at, and there are things that I love and that I'm good at that you don't need or want to love or be good at. Go do all of the things *you* love and that you want to do because that's what's going to make you happy." Soon after that little brotherly pep talk, I started leaning into the idea of being an actress as a career, all because my gem of a brother gave pre-teen Anj a bit of freedom to focus on what *she* really wanted.

Flash forward to my senior year of high school. I had finished all the math classes the school had to offer, so I signed up for Mrs. Chen's advanced math course at the local junior college. I ran into her in the halls of our school one day and she stopped me.

"Anjali, I saw you signed up for my class."

"Yes, I did, Mrs. Chen."

"Why did you sign up for my class?"

"Well, I passed the AP, and there's no more math here, and so I had to sign up for the class you teach at IVC."

"But...you want to be an actress, right?"

"Yes, Mrs. Chen."

"So...why did you sign up for my class?"

Had the answer been, "I have an enduring and passionate love for math, and I just can't bear to be away from it no matter what I choose to do as a career," we would have moved on with our day. But instead, I stammered and stuttered and probably muttered something akin to, "I don't know, because I thought I should." Later I realized, "hey, guess what? Mrs. Chen isn't saying you should or shouldn't take her class. She's letting you know you don't *have to do it all*. In fact, you probably shouldn't if you want to be happy."

If we're lucky, we've been raised to believe that anything is possible for us in this world. Even if we're not so fortunate, there are unlimited books, podcasts, articles, TED talks, Clubhouse rooms, and more telling us we can have whatever we want in life as long as we put our minds to it. As positive and empowering as that message is, at some point, many of us (me, me, me) start to think since we ostensibly *can* have it all, we actually *have* to have it all. We believe if we're good at something, it must mean that's what we have to pursue along with love, family, and riches beyond compare.

That's not true, friends. It's just not.

Don't just take it from me. Michelle Obama talked about the problem with "having it all" in an interview at the Obama Foundation Leaders: Asia-Pacific Program:

> "It's become an interesting mantra in the heads and minds of particularly women. But it's so stupid, just to be honest. No one has it all, and why should we? We're not supposed to have it all. What we fought for as women is choice, the ability to make a broader set of choices for our lives, and where we are now is that there are some people that are judgmental about the choices people make. And for me, I had to come to that realization because trying to have it all just drives you crazy. There was no joy. We have to define that for ourselves. Keep the 'all' thing out of the mix."[2]

I remember having a conversation with my dear friend

Carolina a few years ago, describing how I was doing at a particularly busy period of my year. "Oh, you know how I am," I said, laughing. "I work and work and work my ass off, take on way too many things, then I have a meltdown and crawl into bed for two days and start the whole cycle all over again."

Yeah. *That* sounds healthy. Yet somehow, it's a cycle I've found very hard to break (still working on it).

I think at the core of it is the mutation of a beautiful mindset many of us have been raised to believe: "If I can do it, I have to do it." The healthier version? "Hey I can do any one of these things, just not all at once. So which one do I really want to do?"

This isn't just about overwhelm, though; it's about giving yourself the freedom to decide, "Suppose I *can* have it all, what is it that I actually want?" It's understanding that if you're ordering off the Universal menu, you don't have to order the whole menu. Still to this day, there are communities fighting for the right to *choose* their lives, for the opportunity to simply have options. And so while you are looking at all the things you can do in this world, give yourself permission to say "no" to things, too.

Remember this is your journey, your life. You make the choices. You get to drive. Focus on one dream, go after 20 dreams, your choice. Whether you want a mansion in the Hollywood Hills or a tiny home in the rural Midwest or no

PART 1: IN THE BEGINNING

home at all so you can travel the world—your choice! And yes, for the love of God, you absolutely can change your mind.

Open up that menu and start tasting, ordering meals, and making your own call about what you want out of this big, beautiful life. Just because you can have it all doesn't mean you have to. Choose what lights you up, what makes you feel alive, what gives you joy and purpose and excitement and wonder. It's *your* Fun Size life, so what do you want to order?

CHARLEY LESSON #2: MORE TOYS ALL AT ONCE DOES NOT EQUAL MORE FUN

In the great, "I'm getting a dog and he shall want for nothing, I say...NOTHING" shopping spree of 2010, along with those (much more expensive than they needed to be) lidded garbage cans, I bought an entire crate of adorable toys to keep my little newcomer entertained. I wasn't sure if he was a squeaker or a tugger or a chewer or a pouncer, and I figured I should give him all the tools to discover his own puppy playtime zone of genius.

I have an incredibly adorable video of the first time I played with him and alllllllllll of those toys at once, and I still watch it to this day. He was so young, one of his little chihuahua satellite-dish ears was still floppy, and as he pounced for each toy when I threw it, that ear would flippity-flop along with him, while the other ear stood at full attention ready for duty. You can see this in the video as I throw the furry tiger-patterned squeaky bone and he runs to get it and bring it back, then the chewy rope toy (run, run, run, pounce), then the squeaky monkey (flippity-flop, flop), and the big furry bone pillow. (I mean, clearly these are made for humans to think are cute; ain't no dog thinks that Sherpa fleece thing is a bone.)

And then at one point in the video, there are two toys out in the middle of the room, and he actually grabs both toys with his tiny paws and begins to try to drag them back to the starting line (me). When his mama gets a little overzealous and throws another toy at him, an unexpected thing happens. After a few seconds of trying to drag all three wonderful, magical toys along, he just...gives up. Playtime is over, at least with the toys.

He comes to Mama for snuggles, but what strikes me about this video is that playtime stops being fun when he feels the pressure of trying to do *all* of the things all at once. Yes, he can have it all, just not all at the same time. But the pressure—whether from his own doggie desire or from his unwittingly overzealous mama—to grab all the toys at once made the experience exasperating.

It's just so easy to get caught up in having it all that we forget abundance isn't the acquiring of more, more, more, it's the freedom to choose less. And if we think it's all about grabbing more things, more money, more toys (whether the human kind or the doggie kind), we run the risk of burning ourselves out and making fun time a lot less so.

These days, we stick with one delightful squeaky toy at a time, usually in the form of a squirrel or a stuffed dumpling (inspired by his Uncle Ceddy Lopez, aka the Green Dumpling) that Charley will run after and fetch a good 10 times before tuckering out. And you should see how much he *loves* bringing back that one damn toy every... single... time.

CHOOSING THE PERFECT PATH

As an avid overthinker and deep lover of planning, there have been moments in my life where nothing seemed more agonizing than trying to decide the next right step—whether in my career, my love life, my home life, or even just the next task to take on in the day. I would research and ask a million people their opinions, trusting almost *anyone* besides myself, thinking that somehow the more data I accrued, the more certainty there would be that I could choose the perfect path to the most amazing outcome—to happiness, glory, and calorie-free, dairy-free ice cream.

Yeah, that's never quite worked the way it was advertised in my head. But I'll tell you a story that might make you less worried about choosing the perfect path, and more excited to just *choose*.

In 2013, I was offered a role in Disney's *The Jungle Book*, directed by my beloved friend and colleague Mary Zimmerman, who I knew would make it a masterpiece. (You'll hear much more about Mary and our origin story later.) But the production would take me out of town for six months, which meant I would be away from any potential television or film work for that whole time, not to mention the logistics of Rick's touring schedule meant that we would be apart for the longest period of time ever in our many years together.

I had half the people on my team and in my business telling me I absolutely must go and half of them telling me it was a bad idea. I was driving everyone who was waiting on my decision crazy, including myself.

Ultimately, my heart and my desire to create something beautiful with people I loved won out over the voices around me threatening that it would ruin my career. (Ha!) I finally took the role and made the necessary plans to head out of town, but I was still second guessing myself even after the decision was made. Was I doing the right thing? Were my agents right? Was I going to miss out on something that would have forever changed my life for the better? Were my agents going to fire me? Was my boyfriend going to leave me? The questions went on and on.

Then, I found myself having this conversation (for the thousandth time) with my friend Craig Cady as we were enjoying ourselves at a music festival a few weeks before I was to leave. (Or at least I was attempting to enjoy myself because I was still racking my brain about all the things that may or may not have made this the right decision.) I vomited out all the same old concerns I'd been dropping for the last week or so, and then Craig calmly said these words:

"So, why is this the right decision? Because you've already *made* it. So, it's the right decision."

Other than the fact that my skin isn't goldenrod yellow, at that moment I was an exact replica of the head blown emoji.

🤯

There are no guarantees about the outcome of anything in the future, but by focusing on all the good that *can* come out of a decision we make, we see more and more of the possibilities that present themselves to us along the way. When we are hopeful not fearful, we're open to adventure, excitement, and being pleasantly surprised. And sure enough, once I had recovered from Craig detonating that bomb in my brain, I started to see all the opportunities that could be because I had made this choice.

Looking back, there is nothing but gratitude for the experience of that show—from the first moment I sat in the car to drive across the country with Charley Dog to start rehearsals, to the final moments of saying our goodbyes on closing night.

> **THERE ARE NO GUARANTEES ABOUT THE OUTCOME OF ANYTHING IN THE FUTURE, BUT BY FOCUSING ON ALL THE GOOD THAT CAN COME OUT OF A DECISION WE MAKE, WE SEE MORE AND MORE OF THE POSSIBILITIES THAT PRESENT THEMSELVES TO US ALONG THE WAY.**

I absolutely cannot tell you the secret to choosing the perfect path. What I can tell you is that if you make a choice and move forward without looking back, you have a chance to create not only what you thought you would, but to be wildly and wonderfully surprised by what the Universe drops in your path while you're keeping your eyes open to all the joy that that choice made possible. It's not the outcome that makes it the right choice, it's the choosing and creating from there.

JENNIFER HALE
GUINNESS WORLD RECORDS HOLDER FOR MOST PROLIFIC FEMALE VIDEOGAME VOICE ACTOR, VOICE IN HUNDREDS OF ANIMATED TELEVISION EPISODES, AND ONE INCREDIBLE MOM
WWW.IAMFUNSIZE.COM/JENNIFERHALE

"The most important thing to me as a mom is that my kid is happy....that he can take care of himself, pay his own way, that he's kind, and he's happy he's doing that. It fills him up with joy and he's responsible for himself. And he is just, you know, having fun. Your parents want you to be happy. They do. That is what they want the most. So find your happiness, figure out what makes you happy, and do it, and love it and live it."

PART 1: IN THE BEGINNING

MY FAVORITE ANSWER

When I was growing up, in our beautiful family room with the vaulted ceilings and exposed beam, the main feature for me wasn't the big-screen TV that seemed like the focal point of the room, but the huge built-in shelf filled with books. Books about all subjects—music history, religion, psychology, fiction and non-fiction—a whole wall devoted to learning and the search for answers.

In addition to that epic wall of knowledge, in the den where my parents did all their paperwork and studying was another wall of files, books, and most importantly, a whole shelf containing the holy grail of knowledge: The Encyclopaedia Britannica.* Any time we had a report to do for school, or there was something we wanted to learn more about, my brother and I would head over to this legendary set of tomes within which was contained ostensibly all there was to know (or at least as much of it as could be contained in a series of 26 or so large books with tiny print).

My father was a voracious reader of fiction and non-fiction alike, and so many of those books on that legendary wall were books he had already finished. Whenever I had a

---

*Mind you, young'uns, this was in ye olde tyme before the Internet when, gosh darn it, we actually had to look things up in books and at the library, and yes, I'm slightly embarrassed realizing that half of you reading this book were born well after the Internet was born. So go back in time with me for now and pretend that I'm not quite as ancient as you are perceiving me to be in this moment.

85

question about something in history or politics or medicine or any other subject, I could trust him to not only know something about what I was asking, but to start at the very, very beginning so that I was sure to understand exactly what he was talking about. (As I grew older, this would become a bit of a running joke with the family, but I always loved him for it.) But of all the answers he ever gave me, my absolute favorite, which I heard many times in my younger years, was this one:

"I don't know, let's find out!"

After hearing those words, we'd head to the den to crack open that encyclopedia, or one of the many atlases in the house, or any one of the hundreds of books on that library wall. And we would search for the answer, finding countless tidbits of knowledge along the way.

Those six magical words gave me the tools, emotional and mental, to be an enthusiastic student my entire life. Here was the most knowledgeable person I knew, the man I loved and admired most, admitting that not only did he not know something, but he was excited to find out what the answer was along with me. For him, not knowing wasn't a shameful thing; it was a call to arms, a call to adventure. It meant we could learn something new that day and move into the next one a little fuller than we were before.

So many times, whether at home or in school, or in our lives and careers, we are taught that if we don't know the answer to something, we must be, well...stupid. We believe the message that somehow we are supposed to innately have a knowledge of everything that everyone else our age/background/education level must have, and if we don't, we are somehow at fault for not knowing. Even if we are lucky enough like I was to have someone give us the freedom to explore and learn when we are younger, as we get older/more experienced/more educated, we seem to think the rules change, that not knowing becomes a sign of being unqualified, or worse, unworthy of the position we find ourselves in.

I fell into this trap a lot as an actress early in my career. At one point, I was both delighted and terrified to be working on a show and role that were more challenging to me than any I had taken on up to that point: the role of Lizzie Morden in *Our Country's Good* (so beautifully originated by one of our generation's greatest talents, Cherry Jones).

I remember working on a specific scene and finding myself frustrated and stuck, driving myself crazy because I didn't have the answer, mad at myself for not being able to figure it out. I was a talented actress; how could I not know this? In exasperation, I began asking the director, my classmate Shade Murray, a multitude of questions, and when I finished my laundry list of queries, he happily answered, "I don't know, let's find out!"

God bless Shade and his crazy, curly-haired head, I seriously thought I'd seen my father standing right behind him in that moment, and I almost started crying. I realized I hadn't been chosen for the role because of my knowledge of every single thing about this character. The joy of the experience was to be in the discovery of this show, this person, this story *together* with the cast and crew. I still remember that process as one of my absolute favorites in all of the shows I've done, and one that I am the proudest of, because it was a journey in finding something new and evolving alongside my peers, not just being who I was, showing up, and being more of that person.

Mary Zimmerman has said before that she treats the story and the play she is creating like an archaeological dig. I interpret that to mean we know there is a beautiful artifact there, but we have to be patient and respectful and careful. No rush. No expectation of what it might be because to push it would be to damage it, and to force a meaning or path upon it would be to take away its innate uniqueness and beauty. And that can apply to creating a show or creating your life.

There is no more useful skill than the ability to learn. And we all have it. Think of all the heroes of movies and stories whose ability to learn quickly becomes the very essence of their power—like Neo in *The Matrix* suddenly knowing Kung Fu. As the best-selling author Jim Kwik says in his invaluable book *Limitless*, one of the most important parts of learning is the mindset with which you come at the task.

Jim found himself on the path of teaching people how to

learn after his own struggles as a child. A serious brain injury left him with not only incredible learning challenges, but the words of a careless teacher set him up to potentially feel stunted for life when she said, "That's the boy with the broken brain." Jim had to relearn how to learn. In other words, he had to retrain his own way of thinking about learning, knowledge, and himself. Here's a bit from his book[3] describing that process:

> "Maybe I was asking the wrong question. I started to wonder, what was my real problem? I knew I was a slow learner, but I had been thinking the same way about it for years. I realized that I was trying to solve my learning problems by thinking the way I'd been taught to think—to just work harder. But what if I could teach myself a better method to learn? What if I could learn in a way that was more efficient, effective, and even enjoyable? What if I could learn how to learn faster? I committed in that very moment to finding that way, and with that commitment, my mindset began to shift...I realized that if knowledge is power, then learning is our superpower. And our capacity to learn is limitless; we simply need to be shown how to access it."

Coming from a place of thinking you must know everything or you're stupid does nothing but shut you down. But coming from a place of wonder and excitement sets up your mind and heart to be receptive to the information coming in. If you do not know, you are not broken. You just don't know. Yet. So, on this whole wonderful journey you are on in life, whether it's some kind of factual knowledge or learning something through experience, whether it's a technical skill or a life lesson, don't put that pressure on yourself to already know. Give yourself the gift of wonder and excitement by saying, "I don't know, let's find out."

WHEN IT'S GOOD TO BE BAD AT SOMETHING

I was in 10th grade English class. My teacher, Mrs. Fletcher, had me and another student read an excerpt from the movie script of *Driving Miss Daisy* out loud in class. Naturally, this little Indian girl was asked to read the role of Miss Daisy (mostly because the teacher knew I was a good reader, although the idea of me ever getting to play that role is wrong on so many levels). I read with confidence and gusto, as always, until I got to a particular line where I saw a word I didn't recognize: Episcopalians.

Trusting my general understanding of how to sound out strange words and be right 90% of the time, I boomed out the phrase, "Hanging with the e-pis-CAW-puh-LEE-uns," and about 10 laughing voices shouted out, "e-PIS-co-PAY-lee-uns!" Thankfully, my confidence and general sense of humor allowed me to laugh it off and say, "Okay, now I know. Hey, I'm Hindu." But even without the scar or deep wound of shame that some people carry from moments like this, I still remember it clear as day.

Those moments, for whatever reason, seem to stick. And when they stick in the wrong way, they keep us from wanting to ask questions, to learn, or in the worst cases, to even *try* to learn things for fear of how bad we will look when we start them.

At the beginning of any learning journey, whether you're taking up cooking, a new language, a new school subject, a new sport, a new career, or a new relationship, it's easy to get discouraged by the fear of failure. And almost all of us have a story like mine, a time when we were ridiculed for not knowing something that there was no particular reason we should have known.

Here's the catch, though. Being a beginner is kind of imperative to, ya know, beginning. Being *bad* at something, or at the very least an amateur at it, is actually a very important part of the learning process. The neural pathways that are built during the beginning of any process are some of the strongest and most lasting and vital ones that are created. There is a reason even prima ballerinas go back to the barre daily. It is because the basics are the foundation on which every movement they make are built. And our bodies and minds need those pathways to fire to be able to keep moving along the path to doing more and more complex things.

> **BEING BAD AT SOMETHING, OR AT THE VERY LEAST AN AMATEUR AT IT, IS ACTUALLY A VERY IMPORTANT PART OF THE LEARNING PROCESS.**

In a nutshell, here are four reasons it's great to suck at something at first:

HUMILITY

No one likes a know-it-all, especially when they lord it over the people around them. But everyone roots for the underdog. As I said earlier, my favorite space to be in when learning is that one my father lived in where I have the awareness to say, "I don't know." One giant added bonus is that I get to be an example to others around me who may be afraid of admitting their lack of knowledge, to show them it's 100% okay not to know something and to ask questions and learn.

I remember my college dance teacher, Billy Siegenfeld, talking about starting to study French because, "I like to learn something new every year so I don't forget what it's like to be a beginner at something." As an expert in his craft (and truly, this man is a genius) and a very educated person, he was also aware that the confidence he had from all his knowledge might make it hard for him to put himself in the shoes of the students he was teaching who were just starting. So he put himself in that position regularly to remind him just what it's like to begin again. And again and again.

RECEPTIVENESS

Have you ever been in a conversation where you're talking to someone and they immediately chime in over you as if they've done a dissertation on the topic? It's one of the laughable things about the common experience of mansplaining (or in my world, auntiesplaining or unclesplaining). And it's happened to me enough times that instead of just exiting the conversation as quickly as possible like I used to, I'll stop talking, stare, and then say, "Are you done telling me what I was about to say? Because I'd like to say what I was about to say now." My edges get *sharp*. But as much as this behavior frustrates me, truth bomb: I am *incredibly* guilty of doing it in conversations with people, especially my husband.*

As Jim Kwik says in *Limitless,* one of the biggest blocks to learning is thinking you already know something. When we go into a learning process thinking we know something, or when we read a book, listen to a lecture or a podcast, take a class, or join a conversation thinking, "Yeah, yeah, I know that," we immediately start to selectively listen to or process the information coming in. It's not necessarily a bad thing; our brains are wired specifically to sort and analyze only the information that they deem necessary to our survival. The problem is, the words, "Yeah, yeah, I know," cut us off from new information, ideas, interpretations, and perspectives. Having the mindset of a beginner, even when we aren't, can keep us open to a wider understanding of all kinds of topics and a richer experience with a variety of subjects.

---

*I swear, if he ever reads this book, it's gonna be like 10 sessions of free therapy. He'll realize, "Oh, you know you do that and you're working on it! Okay, no worries then, babe, take your time."

PERSISTENCE

It's been said time and time again that the hardest part of anything is just starting. Not for me. For me, the hardest part of anything is the follow-through. The sticking to it when it's hard, the riding out that discomfort and impatience, the shutting off the noisy judge in my head trying to tell me it's not worth it, when is this going to matter, it's going to take too long to be good at it, and so on. Oh, that damn snarky little voice.

Allowing yourself to be a beginner and pushing through that initial resistance builds that mental muscle within you that says, "Just keep going, you've got this." A huge part of building that muscle, of course, includes actually knowing that there is some kind of reward at the end of the journey. Dr. Andrew Huberman (one of my favorite experts to listen to online, a neuroscientist and Stanford professor of neurobiology who seems to have made a mission of sharing his genius with the world in his "spare" time) has spoken at length about how the neurotransmitters that fire in our brains at any given time can actually support either our "stick-to-it-iveness" or our instinct to quit something. (And if you stick to reading this book, you'll hear more in depth about this in a future section. Aha! Cliffhanger.)

THE JOY OF LEARNING

This is the best part of allowing yourself to be bad at something: the satisfaction and pride of finally getting it, or even starting to. The moment when you're driving down the street, you see a sign in French, and you can read it easily. The moment when you first hit that serve that makes it over the net. These seemingly small achievements have so much more meaning after you've worked for them. Yes, it's fun to be good at something right away, and you can impress friends and family with your innate talent, but there is an incredible satisfaction that comes from having worked hard for something.

One of my favorite childhood memories of practicing piano was when I was working on a particularly frustrating two-measure phrase in a song. I kept going over it and over it and over it until finally, one glorious time, I nailed it. I heard my father's voice come booming out from the den across the house, "THERE you go!" and suddenly I was filled with pride, eagerness, and motivation to keep practicing.

Give yourself the gift of success by being willing to be a failure at something when you start. Trust me, the pride you feel when you *do* get it right is something you'll relish more after knowing where you started.

PART 1: IN THE BEGINNING

ONLY YOU DECIDE WHO YOU ARE

This may be part of what makes me "just the right amount of crazy," as Rick likes to say, but the times in my life when I feel the absolute clearest about my own identity are the times when I am playing a role—or more than one role—for the *most* hours possible in a day. One of the happiest times in my life was when I was playing Juliet by day in a "short Shakespeare" production of *Romeo and Juliet* at Chicago Shakespeare Theatre and doing *The Vagina Monologues* by night at the Apollo Theatre.

On any given day, I was running through just about every emotion and extreme experience I could imagine at the time, and doing it through the eyes and heart of another character. Juliet alone experiences the magic of love at first sight, the grief of losing a loved one, the ecstasy of having sex for the first time, the terror of being effectively disowned by her father, and, the greatest heartbreak of all, ending her own life—all in the span of that one play. (Oof, I suppose I should have given a spoiler alert there, even though it's centuries old. But trust me, knowing the end of that play won't ruin it for anyone, and if you haven't read it or seen Baz Luhrman's glorious film adaptation, get thee to a library or television *immediately*, and bring lots of Kleenex.)

One would think that I would've been utterly emotionally exhausted by the end of a day like that, but instead, after each two-show day, I would find myself energized and renewed, excited to be the very person that I am in real life after having taken these epic journeys through these other lives that were so clearly not mine. The delineation between what I was when I was playing those roles and who I am in my own life was immensely clear. I knew without a doubt when I was seeing the world as them versus as myself. Before, between, and after the shows was *me* time.

I may be an actress, and therefore used to playing a lot of different roles, but the truth is we all play multiple roles in our lives. In our life stories, we get placed in roles from the very beginning—family roles like son/daughter, mother/father, sibling, husband/wife; career roles like boss, employee, manager; personal roles like friend, confidant, caretaker, you name it. We take on so many titles and positions throughout our lives, it's tempting to think those roles are who we actually are. That's why it's so important to take the time, whether a few minutes a day or scheduled time in a week or a whole trip away from people, to connect with who you know yourself to be. That person at your core, your soul, your being, who has dreams and desires and likes and dislikes and passions and purpose. Make time to connect with the source of your, for lack of a better term, you-ness. Where do you find your "you"?

Solitude is one of the most important conditions I have for connecting with that me-ness. It's not that I don't know who I am around other people. It's that I need to be alone to focus on me and only me. It's a known scientific fact that we are energetic beings putting off our own specific vibrations into the world, and for me to connect with who I am, it's important for me to be alone with my unique energy. As a particularly sensitive being, I can't even do this when someone else is in the house, even in another room. I don't need a walkabout or a trip somewhere far away (although I highly recommend those for soul-searching as well). A really well-intentioned walk, drive, or hike, or even sitting alone in my car or in an outdoor open area really helps.

MAKE TIME TO CONNECT WITH THE SOURCE OF YOUR, FOR LACK OF A BETTER TERM, YOU-NESS. WHERE DO YOU FIND YOUR 'YOU'?

There's also the fact that no matter how loving someone may be, how close you are to them, when you're working on making big changes (or even small ones) in your life, it can be hard for those closest to you to hold the space for you to be different than you were a minute ago, a day ago, a month ago. It's honestly one of the biggest challenges I've found to making important changes. The truth is, we can change who we are *whenever we want*, but sometimes the world around us needs time to catch up, to adjust its perception of us.

Are you someone with a bad temper? You could decide right now that you're never going to lose your cool again, but the people around you might still treat you like a person with anger management issues. When I'm working on myself, I am fond of saying to my dear ones, "I need you to hold space for the possibility that I can change, or it's going to be much, much harder for me to fix this." Sometimes those first steps to identifying who we are at our core and who we want to be need to be taken alone in a different environment.

Right now, you might be saying, "Okay, okay, Anj, I'm off on my hike or drive or walk or alone at home. But what exactly am I looking for? Aren't I *always* me?"

Yep, absolutely (or at least one would hope), but when you think about yourself, when you describe yourself even in this moment, what's the first thing you go to? Do you immediately describe yourself physically? Do you talk about your career? Do you talk about your family, your friends? Who you are at your core is something deeper than all that.

Some of the questions I find myself asking to really know who I am at any given moment are more like:

- "What makes me happy?"

- "What makes me righteously indignant enough to want to change the world?"

- "What energizes me? What makes me laugh, sing, jump for joy?"

If you want to go deeper (which I'm all about) forget the questions altogether and just lean into quiet, stillness, and

PART 1: IN THE BEGINNING

whatever you're feeling. Meditation is great for this. Being still, focused on breath, imagery, and sensation, not emptying your thoughts or trying to eliminate your sense of self. While that's a powerful form of meditation for other purposes, your intention now is to connect to raw emotion or sensation or something more ineffable but definitely something that involves joy.

Here's another way to put it, courtesy of the fine creators at Pixar.

Pixar has an uncanny ability to take an animated film and turn it into beautiful life lessons we can all learn from and feel forever altered. *Soul* is one of my favorites from the last few years. (SPOILER ALERT: Skip this and the next paragraph if you haven't seen the movie. I will *not* be unconsciously responsible for ruining that beauty for you.) In the movie, Soul #22 is on the hunt for her "spark": the passion that makes her life worth living. Through a strange and wonderful series of events, she connects with and inhabits the body of Joe, a man who has met a very untimely end before accomplishing what he believes to be his life's purpose—success as a musician. Joe says, "I was born to play," touting, "Music is all I think about. From the moment I wake up in the morning to the moment I fall asleep at night." It's his passion and what he believes to be his life's purpose.

What he and 22 both learn through the course of the movie is that a spark, or a passion, isn't a soul's purpose. No, a soul's purpose is the enjoyment and relishing of every moment, the wonder of new experiences, the compassion or grief or happiness or contentment we feel moment to moment. A passion, a career, a talent, a role, a spark...whatever you want to call it. It isn't your purpose. And it isn't you.

Who you are is a deeply personal thing you don't ever have to share with anyone else. But you *do* need to discover it for yourself. I know I've said I don't want to tell you what to do, and ultimately, it's not my place, my job, or within my power to make you do anything. But, dear reader, I'm going to make a very emphatic suggestion: Take some time with yourself out in the world or in your own home to think deeply about who you are. Look at your environment with new eyes, see what hits you, observe what thoughts come into your head that spark something light and full and wild and wonderful. See if you can, for just a few moments, step out of all those wonderful roles you play and just be you. Revel in that person, that soul. You can (and will) go back to all those roles anytime you want. For now, just revel in being you. The you that you love and know you can be and want to be. Unabashedly, effortlessly you.

PART 1: IN THE BEGINNING

CRISPIN FREEMAN

PROLIFIC VOICE ACTOR (OVERWATCH, YOUNG JUSTICE, NARUTO) AND VOICE ACTING COACH, HOST OF THE VOICE ACTING MASTERY PODCAST, MYTHOLOGY SCHOLAR, DEVOTED HUSBAND, AND WONDERFUL FRIEND

WWW.IAMFUNSIZE.COM/CRISPINFREEMAN

"Ask yourself: the people who love you in your life, do they love you because of what you do, because of what you have, or because of what other people think about you? The answer is no. If they truly love you, it's not based on any of these three things. So what's left? YOU! There's a part of you that they love that obviously has nothing to do with what you do, what you have, or what other people think about you. And that lovable part of you is very big! The revelation is that you're lovable, not because of those three things that your ego might be concerned with, but because of the deeper part of you."

CHARLEY LESSON #3: IF YOU LISTEN, I WILL TELL YOU WHAT I NEED.

It was day one of Charley coming home—well, night one—and we were about to snuggle into our respective beds. I was crate training him, and he seemed to already be in love with his little nook, but I still didn't completely trust that, puppy that he was, he would be able to get through the night without needing to go out. That said, I also had no idea how puppies conveyed that information to their owners. Would he let me know or just have an accident in his crate and be silently miserable until I woke up in the morning?

So I did the only thing I knew how to do: I sat him down and had a little conversation with him. Looking at his cute little face on the corner of my bed, I said, "Okay, little guy, I'm gonna make you a deal. I don't care if it's 3:00 in the morning or 3:00 in the afternoon, I promise, if you need to go out, I will drop everything I am doing to take you out. But you have to tell me. I don't know how you're gonna do it, but you have to tell me in a way I can understand. You just let me know and I've got you, okay?"

Now, having never been a dog owner in my life, I had no

idea what to expect here. And yes, the idea that he would understand a word of what I had said was a bit...well, ya know, Doctor Dolittle-y. But somehow, sure enough, at 3:31 that morning (yes, I remember it that precisely), a tiny little whimper came from that crate and I leapt out of bed with joy, saying, "Good boy! Good boy, Charley! Thank you for telling me!" as I scooped him up and ran out the door with him. If there was anyone on the street that night, I can't imagine what they were thinking, seeing this crazy little lady so happy to see her dog taking a leak in front of the building. But I knew in that moment, he would always tell me what he needed, and I would always listen.

Huh, now *there's* a lesson that can probably be applied to our own souls. (*Oof. How's that for a little realness, Anj?*) How often have you heard a tiny voice inside you whimpering that you need something, and you've drowned it out with the "shoulds" or the "can'ts" or the "No, no, nos." I know I've done it more times than I care to admit, which reminds me of this very, very special lesson I learned from Charley. And now I can never forget it.

How the Hell Do I Love Myself?

Steel yourself. I'm about to curse. A lot.

For someone who has read what feels like an entire library of self-help books in her lifetime, there are certain things I've come across time and time again that make me, well, vomit a little in my mouth. Or cringe. Or roll my eyes. Or all three at once, which is *not* something you want to see.

Years ago, in much darker times, that eye-rolling was mostly frustration at not having any clue how to do the things I was being told I "had" to do, one of the most ubiquitous and annoying being: "You have to learn to love yourself..." followed by the even *more* annoying: "...before you can love anyone else."

Whenever I heard those words, the tirade in my head would go something like this*: (heavy, heavy sigh) Are you FUCKING KIDDING me? What does that even MEAN? "Love" myself? I don't even LIKE myself. And besides, how do I just DO that? And now you're telling me I'm totally fucked for all relationships until I figure this out? Why won't anyone tell me what that MEANS???*

Yeah. It pissed. Me. OFF. And it made me dislike myself even more for not knowing what it looked like, or felt like, or even how to figure out how to love myself. Well, I'll say it here: I figured it out. And I know relationship advisors, life coaches, therapists, psychologists, mothers, friends, and I'm sure some small animals would all gasp in shock at what I'm about to say, but stick with me, friends, and I swear there's not only a payoff; there's a happy ending. Eventually my new, highly evolved response to that pithy mandate I and so many others are told we *have* to follow became:

"The fuck I do."

Okay, mostly that is my response to being told what to do in general. But also, I've loved plenty of people in my life, and only one of them showed up at the time when I had "learned to love myself," or at least barely started to see what it sort of meant to love myself. (Thankfully, he stuck around as I figured it out and cheered me on as I did.) I will say, however, life has become a hell of a lot more fun now that I understand what that means to me.

So, how did I figure out the answer to this $100-million question?

Simple. I got a dog.

I'm not saying you need to go out and get a dog to learn to love yourself. Adopting an animal is a deep and abiding commitment to another creature, and it's not a decision to be taken lightly. For me, though, getting a dog was probably the best decision I ever made in my entire life because Charley was the greatest harbinger of marvelous things I could have ever asked for. But several years into dating my husband, at one of the times when I was most frustrated by hearing ye olde adage that I had to love myself before I could love someone else (because, again, I cry bullshit) I had one of those moments that felt like a lightbulb had literally gone off inside my brain. My eyes blinked open and my ears felt all tingly.

All I had to do to know how to love myself was look at how I treated my Charley, that sweet little furry bodhisattva that carried my heart around with his four tiny paws. It didn't matter if there was a bone sticking out of my leg, that little guy would be walked, fed, cared for, and loved beyond all measure.

Before that lightbulb moment, I wasn't doing a very good job of loving myself. I would research raw food diets and order organic grain-free puppy food while eating Pop Chips for dinner. I would make sure to get him out and walked, but I would skip the gym or hike or any workouts because, "Meh, I look fine." I would listen intently to his many sounds and even the different ways he would breathe for signs of what he needed and hop out of a deep sleep to take him out in the middle of the night based on the slightest whimper. Meanwhile, I would willfully ignore my own gut instinct on things, trusting instead almost anyone else's opinions over my own.

If Charley had an accident (which was so rare, I mean, this dog would rather go into kidney failure than pee in the house), even if I was annoyed or upset, I would never call him "bad dog," but the things I would say to myself when I disappointed myself (which felt so often) would make your hair curl. I didn't know how to love myself, but by God, I knew how to love this dog.

And guess what? I knew how to love my boyfriend really well, too. I watched and listened and sensed and felt and did everything I could to create a world for him where he felt like the king he was. No matter where he was or what was happening around him, I made sure he felt supported and heard and lifted up and, yes, occasionally, given a rather hard-core talking-to when it was something that might help him. He did the same for me, but I hadn't learned to do the same for myself.

So, basically, I learned how to love myself by watching the way I was loving others. I discovered that love is paying attention. Love is doing what's necessary to give someone—including yourself—the biggest, fullest life possible. No matter the circumstances, no matter the date, no matter the mood. It's an action, not just a feeling. It's a verb, not just a noun. Loving yourself is paying attention to your needs, your desires, your dreams, your intuition, your fears, your triumphs, your weaknesses, and giving yourself what you need to create more of the good and learn from the bad. Even when you don't want to. When you're tired. When you're sad. When it feels hopeless. No matter what.

You can love yourself even when you don't like yourself. I would argue you should love yourself even *more* when you don't like yourself because it takes an awful lot of positive reinforcement and support to remember who you truly are when you think you're not worthy of love, or when you are feeling low, lost, confused, or any number of difficult-to-navigate emotions.

LOVING YOURSELF IS PAYING ATTENTION TO YOUR NEEDS, YOUR DESIRES, YOUR DREAMS, YOUR INTUITION, YOUR FEARS, YOUR TRIUMPHS, YOUR WEAKNESSES, AND GIVING YOURSELF WHAT YOU NEED TO CREATE MORE OF THE GOOD AND LEARN FROM THE BAD.

All that insight came from loving my tiny, furry, snuggly, perfect little boo and his unbearably adorable face. He really is like a furry little Buddha.

THE CANDY-COATED SHELL

Ever since I can remember, my size has always been a part of how other people describe me. My family nickname was Jaadu (meaning "chubby," thanks to my baby cheeks, a pet name that stuck well into my adult years) and other people would call me small, little, or Shrimp. Those little legs were also not particularly fast, so I also earned the nickname Turtle on my third-grade soccer team. Turtle, Chubby, and Shrimp. Excellent.

Then in fourth grade, I was, shall we say, "blooming early." A group of sixth-grade girls, likely jealous but possibly just needing an easy target, named me "Bongo Boobs." Still, I stayed unfazed, knowing these were descriptors, some accurate, some more subjective, and yes, a few intended to hurt. But none were a *definition* of me; none were who I was. They were all just...a description.

Then I got to high school—that magical, insane time when the pressure to achieve battles with the pressure to fit in (along with hormones and rather new feelings about other people you aren't entirely sure how to handle), and you get lost in your many identities. Add that to my love of acting, and it was a recipe for those descriptors to start turning into definitions.

As I started to audition, it was hard to ignore the fact that I was always being cast as (or rejected because I was) "the short one," "the dark one," "the tiny one," "the not-blue-

Part 1: In The Beginning

eyed one." Sadly, I began to connect those descriptors to narratives about who I actually was as a person: "I *am* the short, dark one, and all the popular girls are taller/fairer/thinner/prettier. That's why boys will never like me." Given that I was growing up in Orange County, California, where there was little proof that blonde hair and blue eyes were actually *recessive* genes, it felt like a logical conclusion. I was being cast as similar things onstage to what I was being told in life, so they must all be right.

When in my senior year of high school, after committing myself to the school drama program with intense fervor for four years and spending all my creative time becoming a better actress, I wasn't allowed to play even a decent supporting role in the school play because, "Let's be honest, you're short, Anjali. This play is about Amazon warriors. You can't play a big role." It felt like a smack in the face that I interpreted as, "It doesn't matter how good you are, you're always going to look like this, and 'this' isn't good enough."

The more time I spent in front of the mirror (at home or in dance class), the more the image looking back at me became my explanation for why unwanted circumstances abounded in my life. "If only I were prettier, taller, thinner, lighter…," a narrative supported heavily by the magazines of the '90s promising both popularity and a better dating life if I just achieved the "perfect" body (whatever that actually was).

Now, it's all too clear to me how, for so much of my life (and I'm pretty sure I'm not alone), I believed this flesh-and-blood construct that I used as my vehicle on the road of life was the main indication of *who* I was and what was possible for me. I look back now and realize not only how sad that is but how inaccurate. Okay yes, this body wasn't gonna lead me to a life as a professional basketball player, and I wasn't about to be cast as, say, Laurie in *Oklahoma!*, but those weren't things I cared about. But sadly, back then, whether I cared about those things or not, what I *did* care about was what I thought this body I was in meant about *me*.

> **I AM MY THOUGHTS, MY IDEAS, MY SENSE OF HUMOR. I AM MY BELIEFS, MY COMPASSION, MY GENEROSITY. MY BODY? IT'S JUST A SHELL (A BRIGHT, BEAUTIFUL, CANDY-COATED SHELL) THAT CARRIES ALL THAT DELICIOUSNESS AROUND.**

Just like I don't get into my little red 2009 Prius and think I *am* my car, why would I think I *am* my body? Maybe others make judgments about who I am based on my appearance (or my car) but *I know better*. I am my thoughts, my ideas, my sense of humor. I am my beliefs, my compassion, my generosity. My body? It's just a shell (a bright, beautiful, candy-coated shell) that carries all that deliciousness around. Sure, the tasty, crunchy, colorful shell on an M&M is fun, but it's nowhere near the best part. It's what's inside that shell—chocolate, peanut butter, crispy rice, peanuts, you name it—that brings delight.

This outer shell of ours, attractive as it may be, is just that—a candy-coated shell. We can do all the things we want to its appearance or function, just like we can pick pretty much any color of M&Ms these days. We can choose to dress up or dress down, wear makeup or not, fix our hair however, and do whatever we feel is an expression of what makes us happy and feel good. And yes, we do have to take good care of it and not let it fall into disrepair, just like we have to change the oil and check the tires regularly on our vehicle of choice.

But on those days when we look at our appearance and are tempted to think it defines our present or determines the possibility of happiness, joy, success, and love in the future, remember, we don't eat M&Ms for the shell. It's that delicious filling that makes the candy so... damn... good.

PART 1: IN THE BEGINNING

MELA LEE
VOICE ACTRESS (APEX LEGENDS, MIRACULOUS LADYBUG, MORTAL KOMBAT 11), SINGER, SONGWRITER, GOOD SAMARITAN, AND HUGE-HEARTED HUMAN
WWW.IAMFUNSIZE.COM/MELALEE

"Anyone [reading] this, you are beautifully, wonderfully, exquisitely made. You are made of unicorn tears and the laughter of angels, and just the fact that you're here is a miracle. This time is yours. This day is yours. These dreams are yours. I wish when I was younger I had been there for myself. Back then, I would let other people's words define who I was, even though most of them were wrong.

We're in a really beautiful time right now where we get to celebrate our diverse backgrounds, but [coming from] somewhat of a multicultural background, I heard it from both sides that I wasn't enough of something. You are beautifully, wonderfully, exquisitely made. You are worth celebrating every day like it's a holiday."

ENJOYING THE QUEST

Confession time again: The lesson in this chapter is one I keep having to learn over and over. Just weeks ago, I was having a conversation with a coach of mine who was helping me in a particular venture. I was telling him about all the things I was working on—the challenges I was facing, the overwhelm I was feeling, the panic that was setting in, the various solutions I had been implementing that weren't working, etc.—and he had one simple question for me.

"Anjali, are you having fun?"

(Cue the sound of a record player screeching to a stop.)

It's so easy when we are on this journey of life, finding our way and learning new things, to be so caught up in taking in information that we forget to be proud of the fact that we have taken on such a mission. It takes a lot to decide to improve yourself in some way or another. Don't get so focused on the finish line that you forget to relish the process.

I frequently find myself in a phase of devouring information from books and guidance from teachers, filling up notebooks, making notes in the margins, spending all my free time listening to podcasts because, frankly, I love being a student. The challenge I face in these knowledge-seeking spurts is remembering to experience the *joy* in learning something new. I forget to pause and ask myself if I am actually processing all the information I'm taking in.

During one particularly charged time of mental overflow in my life, my sweet Rick said these words to me, "Baby, you gotta make sure you're enjoying the quest. There's gotta be some sense of pride and joy in the fact that you're questing for something bigger. Because that in and of itself is something special to be proud of. Enjoy it."

Oh yeah. Joy. Remember that? Remember *fun*?

The word quest is such a fantastic word because it conjures up images of sorcery and wonder, knights and fair maidens (or kickass maidens who can ride a horse and joust and take on an enemy army). Fantasy fiction is a great source of joy in my life. So thinking about my life as a quest, or a series of quests, is a truly excellent (dare I say *fun*?) way to face the challenges and successes of life.

As you move along on your own quest, think of me as your bardic companion, singing songs and telling tales while you make your own way and fight your own dragons because *you* are the hero in your story. Be proud of yourself every time you take on a new quest, a new mission, or a new journey toward learning something new or improving yourself—not because everyone deserves a medal, but because improving ourselves and learning more is a noble feat. Taking on difficult challenges and surmounting them is something to take pride in. And even though I forget sometimes, having fun isn't just, ya know, fun; it's actually one of the most powerful states to create from. It's wildly energizing. You deserve to have a great time while you traverse the territory inside yourself to learn more, be more, do more.

The quest we're each on is noble. It is long and magical and difficult and maddening and ultimately the most important story of your life. So please, dear reader, enjoy it. And be proud you're here. I sure am. This is going to be an epic adventure.

PART 1: IN THE BEGINNING

JASON RITTER
ACTOR (KEVIN (PROBABLY) SAVES THE WORLD, JOAN OF ARCADIA, GRAVITY FALLS), GUINNESS WORLD RECORD HOLDER FOR MOST HUGS GIVEN IN ONE MINUTE BY AN INDIVIDUAL, NEW FATHER, AND ALL AROUND TALENTED AND SUPER-KIND DUDE
WWW.IAMFUNSIZE.COM/JASONRITTER

"I would tell my younger self not to worry so much about what other people thought about me. I initially tried to kind of fit in everywhere and tried to sort of act like this group of people or that group of people and just try to sort of assimilate, and I wish I had just allowed myself to not shave off all my little weird corners and edges. Because once you get out of elementary school, high school, all of that stuff, you start to find there are more people like you. There are so many different types of people on Earth, and I think people are much more accepting of all of our weird stuff when we get a little bit older. And a lot of times, people can get that stuff scared out of them, and I don't recommend that. So stay weird."

HEY!

NO, THERE'S NOTHING WRONG WITH YOUR EYES. I'M USING THIS HUGE PRINT TO GET YOUR ATTENTION (AND SO YOU CAN PUT THE BOOK DOWN AND STILL SEE IT).

IT'S TIME TO PLAY.

DID YOU DO SOMETHING SILLY OR MAKE YOURSELF LAUGH TODAY?

DID YOU PICK UP A GAME WITH A FRIEND AND LET YOURSELF DIVE IN?

DID YOU DO A SILLY DANCE WALKING DOWN THE STREET? OR A FUNNY WALK?

DID YOU MAKE RIDICULOUS FACES FOR NO REASON?

DID YOU SING AT THE TOP OF YOUR LUNGS?

DID YOU PLAY WITH A PUPPY OR KITTY OR LITTLE KID?

DID YOU PLAY?

AND NOW, A SLIGHTLY MORE SERIOUS EXPLANTION OF WHY IT'S VITAL YOU DON'T FORGET TO PLAY

In addition to the obvious truth that playing is fun, the fact is, it's an absolutely vital part of being a human. I'll make up silly songs while talking to the dog. I'll use weird voices when I'm talking to myself and others. I'll do strange walks down the street (and no, it's not just because I'm nuts). In our constant desire to be productive or successful, it's really easy to think that play is frivolous, unnecessary, and a waste of time. I often say, "I take my fun very seriously," and it's true because we don't have time *not* to have a little play in our lives. Without play, we just don't function well as humans.

It's in our genes to play. In his book, *Essentialism: The Disciplined Pursuit of Less*[4] (one of my favorites from the last 10 years), Greg McKeown spends a whole section talking about the necessity of play:

> "When we play we are engaged in the purest expression of our humanity, the truest expression of our individuality. Is it any wonder that often the times we feel most alive, those that make up our best memories, are moments of play? Play expands our minds in ways that allow us to explore: to germinate new ideas or see old ideas in a new light. It makes us more inquisitive, more attuned to

novelty, more engaged...Or as Albert Einstein once said: 'When I examine myself and my methods of thought, I come to the conclusion that the gift of fantasy has meant more to me than my talent for absorbing knowledge.'"

Think about how fully engaged you are when you're playing something you really enjoy. Whether it's a video game, a board game, sports, or playing pretend with your little sister, there is a part of your brain that kicks into high gear. As McKeown says, "Play stimulates the parts of the brain involved in both careful, logical reasoning *and* carefree, unbound exploration."

No matter how serious life gets, no matter what is going on in our world, no matter how dire it may seem, no matter how much work we have to get done, there is no time for us *not* to play. We need it to release endorphins, to reframe our mindset, to reset stress levels, and of course, to have *fun*.

So give yourself a break. Give your brain a little treat. Hike. Sing. Laugh. Play a board game with a friend or your niece or nephew. Get online with some friends and try out that new role-playing game you've been hearing about. (I maintain that RPGs are seriously one of the most powerful educational and bonding tools we have on the planet. Nothing is quite as satisfying to me as playing with a bunch of people who take their fun as seriously as I do.) Give your brain that delicious sustenance it needs by allowing it to fire in a different and wonderful way. Play, play, play, play, play.

PART 1: IN THE BEGINNING

"YOU'RE DOING A GREAT JOB. BE KIND TO YOURSELF AND HAVE FUN."

— JENNIFER HALE

Part 2

The Messy Middle

"IF YOU'RE GOING THROUGH HELL, KEEP GOING."
— WINSTON CHURCHILL

WHEN LIFE HAPPENS...

It can (and often does) happen to anyone, in any story, in any life, any creative process, any new endeavor. You are on your way, gaining momentum, energized by your initial successes, when you slam into an obstacle or slump into a lull of discouragement. And you begin to wonder why you ever thought this was a good idea to start with.

I remember a particular one of those moments so vividly. It was a few days into tech rehearsals for a play of we were remounting in Seattle after a successful run in Princeton. I had spent the break between with my boyfriend at the time, working through some rather large issues we were having in our relationship. Where I had felt despondent going into that break, after our talks, I was at least feeling hopeful, and I had come to Seattle with a renewed sense of vigor and purpose.

I was leaving the theatre one night with a large box of goods I had sent ahead containing books and workout clothes and other items I knew I would need during the run of the show. I was going to be active and busy and focused on being brilliant in the production, and then go back feeling physically and mentally clear and triumphant, back into my boyfriend's proud and loving arms. And as I walked happily out the theatre door and down the street to my very close apartment...

SNAP.

I hadn't even clocked that the curb was there, and my ankle rolled so hard stepping off it that I thought it must have broken. "No, no, no, no." I said out loud, thinking, "Not now, please, not when things were just about to get better. Not right before we start the show. Not now, not now."

It seems to happen like clockwork. You're all set to take on a new goal. You've put everything in place to conquer it. You're on the path. You're enjoying the quest. You've got pep in your step and fire in your belly when—boom. Life happens. Something gets in the way. We're not talking about a little speed bump. We're talking an entire construction zone that derails your plan.

I'm not being negative here. I'd be hard-pressed to think of a time I cruised down a smooth, detour-free road toward something I deeply wanted to accomplish. A lot of times, it's a *big* challenge that pops up to knock me off my axis. And then, of course, the lamenting and frustration and demoralization sets in, and suddenly, I'm back in the mire where I started before I even set the goal in the first place.

Life is always going to keep happening while we are pursuing our goals. That may sound ridiculously simplistic to say, but it's true. Life never takes a break, which means no matter how much we focus, how much woo-woo we practice, how much manifesting and meditating and planning and dreaming we do, there *will* be challenges. Those challenges will range from mildly annoying to, unfortunately, giant hurdles that truly require us to put our dreams on hold.

I've come across both ends of the spectrum and everything in between. This is life, folks. And while I do believe there is a deeply loving and supportive Universal force out there conspiring with us to create the life of our dreams, I also know that sometimes, things are going to happen in ways and at times that are wildly inconvenient.

It happened in the most shocking of ways when I began to write this book. I had finally set aside real time to write, I had cleared my calendar and actually said no to enough things to have room in my schedule to create. I had all the ideas on Post-it Notes lined up on the wall like little soldiers. I had stocked up on coffee and mechanical pencils and legal pads. I was ready to go. And then, out of nowhere, my vibrant, brilliant mother had a freak accident and ended up in the emergency room with a major head injury. (I could spend the rest of this book talking about all the ways and reasons I love my mom, but I won't only because I wouldn't be able to type through the tears.)

For the next three weeks, she was in and out of the hospital, alternating between being in severe pain and fighting extreme nausea, or on high doses of painkillers to provide relief and let her rest. She eventually had to have surgery, with a neurosurgeon burring holes into her skull to relieve the pressure on her brain from the bleeding. Our whole family rallied to be with her. We focused every thought, every ounce of our energy, every moment of our days and nights on her recovery.

Now, my mom is one of the very people I wrote this book for, and frankly, I do most everything in my life with her in mind one way or the other. I wouldn't be who or where I am in the world without her. While we were at each other's throats in my teenage years (like most mothers and daughters), in adulthood, she has become a vital part of my everything.

When her accident happened, though, not only was this book nowhere on my radar, but suddenly, my whole life was upside down. I lost my mooring completely. I couldn't think straight, at least not until we were sure she was out of the woods. All I could focus on was Mom, and once the extreme danger was past, it was like I had been hit by a truck myself. I just crashed. Hard.

I'm happy to report that the biggest challenge with Mom now is getting her to relax. She has returned to full and vibrant health, and since she had so much downtime, she thinks she has to make up for lost time. Last time we visited, she was on the exercise bike. At 82. After brain surgery. She is unstoppable, thank God.

I, however, had stopped dead in my tracks. And as the danger subsided, I had not only lost my momentum, I was beating myself up for not staying on task, for missing my self-imposed deadlines, for failing her and myself. *You were doing so well and now you've dropped the ball... again.*

Thankfully, I didn't let the negative self-talk last long this time. I quickly turned myself around to say, *Nope, Anjali.*

Nope, nope, nope. It's okay. Life. Happens. And what do you do about it? Keep... on... going. Go slowly if you have to, but go.

You know what all those self-flagellating thoughts *weren't* helping me do? Write this book. As soon as I took a moment to have some self-compassion, to honor what my family and I had just been through as well as the graceful way we came together in love and support and positivity, I was filled with renewed passion and excitement to get back on the writing train. After all, I had just seen how fragile life can be. And how many times had I thought, *I just want Mom to see this book out in the world?* This was the *perfect* time for a new beginning.

When we come across construction zones or completely washed-out sections of the road to our goals, the first step is knowing we haven't done anything wrong by stopping and dealing with the issue at hand. Losing momentum or diverting plans isn't a failure. Often, it's a choice. Sometimes something else will *and should* take priority.

Second, know there is value in pausing to look where that detour is diverting you, in asking yourself if there is opportunity along the path it is setting you on. While you're laid up with that ankle, recovering from that stomach bug, dealing with that flood in your apartment, or stranded after your flight was cancelled, is there something else you can work on? Can you take the time in bed to catch up with old friends via email? Can you educate yourself more on nutrition and begin getting comfortable with a new eating program before you start it? Can you use the time to take on another goal you had to put on the shelf while you were focusing on this one?

Sometimes it doesn't matter which goal you're working towards as long as you are working on one. Momentum breeds momentum. And if you find yourself stuck in one lane, sometimes it's great to change lanes and get moving forward in another one. Inertia works both ways—an object at rest does require a tremendous force to get it moving, but on the flip side, an object in motion is more likely to stay in motion unless acted upon by a tremendous force to stop it. So even if your plans take a hit, one of the best ways to keep that momentum going is to say with excitement and enthusiasm, "Okay, how is this going to work in my favor?" or "Okay, how is this going to get me to where I want to be?"

"What? Anj, be real here. I just sprained my freakin' ankle, and I was planning on running a marathon. How the hell is this supposed to help me get where I want to be?"

Well, turn the page and let me tell you another story while you rest, ice, and elevate that swollen little paw of yours.

"WHAT YOU RESIST PERSISTS...PUNCHES YOU IN THE FUCKING FACE"

My dear friend and mentor, Cathleen Campbell Stone, has an excellent way of taking platitudes and turning them into something that actually hits home. I remember a conversation with her that went like so:

"Anj, c'mon, you know the saying: What you resist..."

"I know, I know (heavy eye roll): persists."

"And you know what it does if you keep resisting?"

"What?"

"It punches you in the fucking face."

Truer words were never spoken, Cathleen.

When I was in college, despite my passion for acting and singing, I found myself leaning further and further into dance. I loved it. I loved my teacher, the aforementioned dynamic and brilliant Billy Siegenfeld. I loved the company he was building and bringing me into. It made me feel truly alive. I was still doing musicals and plays, but I was also spending anywhere from three to six hours a day in dance class and rehearsals, which was a pretty clear commitment to pursuing this path after graduation.

I knew I wanted to be a performer. I loved acting and wanted to be an actress, but somehow dancing had begun to take up more and more of my time and focus. The little voice in my head that said, *What about...* to my other dreams was drowned out by, *But look how well this is going. Everybody else says this is what you should do.*

Then one day, while we were rehearsing, during one of the simplest moves in the whole number, my knee just...well...snapped. Bent sideways. And suddenly, I couldn't straighten my leg. I won't go into the gory details here, but the long and the short of it is, I had torn the lateral meniscus on my knee and needed surgery. *No big deal*, I thought. *Bump in the road. Arthroscopic surgery has a recovery time of like six weeks. I'll be back at 'em in no time.*

Well, since I don't seem to do anything half-assed in my

life, surgery revealed there wasn't just a little tear in my meniscus; I had torn it completely off the bone. Recovery time went from six weeks to six months. I remember the doctor very bleakly telling me not only would I never dance again, it was unlikely I'd be able to even run or walk normally again.

At the time, my determined little self immediately replied, "Oh, yeah, no. That's not...I mean, thank you, but you're wrong. That's not gonna happen." Okay, actually in my head I believe the words were, *The fuck I won't,* but I was raised to respect my elders, especially doctors. Still, I'd like to point out here that I was in fact right. If you've met me any time in the last 20 years, you know what that doctor had spoken over me was B.S. I was *not* accepting that prognosis.

However, the long recovery time *was* going to throw a giant wrench into the works. Six months of not dancing, at least a month of not really walking, several months in a full leg brace (in the Chicago winter, oof)—this was *not* what I signed up for. But it was what happened.

There were definitely some not-so-graceful moments (physically and emotionally), but you know what? Overall, I didn't let the injury stop me. Here's what I remember of that time:

In the first few days of recovery, I distinctly remember thinking, *So what can I do during this time? I've been really bad at keeping in touch with friends and family that don't live here. I can use this time to love on them more. Once I can hobble around with this cast, I can go to the gym and train the rest of my body.* (I also happened to work at my gym as a personal trainer and front desk gal at the time, so thankfully, I could still make a little money while I was pivoting.) *And in the meantime, I'm just gonna see what pops up.*

The first time I returned to the studio to just watch my dance company rehearse, I felt immense love for my peers as they moved gracefully, lightly, powerfully all over the stage. But I also felt an incredible sadness because somehow I knew, just *knew*, I wouldn't be coming back. When I spoke to Billy afterwards, through tears, I said to him, "I'm just so sad because I don't know how I'm going to ever get the feeling back—the one I get when I'm dancing with you all. There's nothing else I have in the world that makes me feel that way, and I don't know what I'm going to do."

I can't remember if it was weeks or months later, but very soon after I was finally brace-free, walking mostly without pain, I auditioned for a show at the Goodman Theatre called *Mirror of the Invisible World*, directed by a woman named Mary Zimmerman. (See? Told ya the origin story was coming.) The audition was the first I'd done for any theatre since graduating college the previous summer. I'd been so focused on dance and then out of commission since the injury, I'd completely lost sight of my first love: Acting.

It was a delightful audition, and this Mary lady just felt...joyful. Someone who wasn't sitting on the other side of that casting table waiting to be impressed, she was eager to be entertained. She didn't want to just work, she wanted to *play*. And to make sure the actors in front of her were enjoying it, too.

I booked that job. And suddenly, my path was adjusted back to what had been my focus since middle school. I went on to do 18 different productions with Mary (who remains one of the many angels in my life. I can't thank her enough for her friendship, guidance, and belief in me), including one show that changed my life forever, *Metamorphoses*. This show, adapted from Ovid's epic poem, was a series of ancient myths all based around the concept of change, of the metamorphoses of souls of all kinds—joyful, tragic, redemptive.

We performed that show all over the country and then came to New York right before 9/11, opening on Broadway in 2012. It was a balm for so many souls who were feeling the pain of senseless tragedy, who were needing to find light and hope for the future without denying the truth of what they were feeling and experiencing in the now. I could write a whole chapter—probably a whole book—about that experience.

To this day, people come up to me on the street, at restaurants, all over the place to tell me how much that show meant to them. And I tell them not only, "Thank you," but, "I understand," because it meant so much to *me*. Like all of Mary's shows (but somehow this one felt more so than the others I had done because of her beautiful style of combining movement and imagery with traditional acting), I was able to connect my love of movement and dance, and the skills I had developed in all those years with Billy, to my love of storytelling.

If I had let that knee injury stop me, if I hadn't trusted that the pivoting I was doing was going to work out in the end, if I hadn't kept that forward momentum going just by training and seeing what came next, I could have spiraled my way into thinking this was just a story of broken dreams. Instead it was a story of making a forgotten dream come true, indeed of combining that dream with an even greater one: the melding of these art forms I loved so much. Billy always said in class, "You don't have to be 'dancers.' You're people—people who dance." My injury had allowed this to be truer for me than ever.

And as for my love of dancing? Oh, I haven't stopped that at *all*. I've danced on television, on Broadway, and in countless live music venues all over the world, onstage and off. But it's been in service of the bigger picture: a career in the passion I've always had. That has brought me more joy than you can possibly imagine.

Just remember: When you have a goal, but life happens on the way, be kind to yourself. Be patient. But most of all, just... keep... moving. You've got this.

Anjali Bhimani

Before Takeoff, a Quick Reminder to Put on Your Oxygen Mask First

Many, many years ago, I found myself drowning in a relationship with a loving, kind, talented, truly wonderful man. We would spend our weekends hanging around the living room belting out Matchbox 20 songs. We talked for hours and hours about our love of theatre and performance. I still remember when we were doing a show together on the West Coast and we took a trip to the ocean, which he had never seen before that day, having spent his whole life in the Midwest. Watching him and reveling in his glee at seeing seals on the rocks and putting his feet in the

Pacific for the very first time filled me with such love, and it warms my heart to this day. We were the best of friends.

But, this wonderful man was also wrestling some very dark demons at the time. I spent years of our relationship doing my absolute best to support him, to show him what I saw—what I knew the *world* saw—in him. But those demons were very, very powerful.

I wanted so badly for him to prevail against his demons, but as I battled alongside him, I struggled to maintain my own light, to maintain enough energy to pull him up the ladder instead of letting myself be pulled down. Eventually, I realized my life was becoming less and less about the needs of this sweet man than of his demons. I was feeling smaller and smaller. I began battling voices of my own that were dark and unfamiliar. The more I let my own self-care slide and centered my world around his demons, the deeper I fell into that hole with him.

It slowly started to dawn on me that maybe instead of bravely fighting the battle for him, I was selfishly standing in the way of him getting the help he truly needed at the time. I was down in the hole with him, struggling to hold him just above rock bottom, realizing that rock bottom might be exactly where he needed to be for a minute. Not only that, I was feeling closer and closer to the point when I wouldn't be able to find my own light again. In short, I was trying to secure his oxygen mask first, and we were both suffocating.

Still, when I finally had the strength to end the relationship, I was exploding with self-loathing. How could I leave this person who loved me and needed me so much? How could I leave when he was so low? I called several of his friends before the breakup asking them to please, please, please help him and take care of him through this time. It was a terrible decision to have to make. And in the moment, I couldn't be 100% sure it was the right one. All I knew was that I needed an oxygen mask or we would both lose the battle.

I WAS TRYING TO SECURE HIS OXYGEN MASK FIRST, AND WE WERE BOTH SUFFOCATING.

To say this period of separating was excruciating would be a wild understatement. I wasn't exactly financially flush at the time, so I sought out every free or discounted resource I could find (and shared some with his friends in hopes of guiding him toward them as well). I found a therapist on a sliding scale to help me find my way out of hating myself for choosing my well-being first. I began to rock climb more (because you can't listen to bullshit voices in your head when you're doing everything you can not to plunge to your death). I read fiction—*not* self-help—because I needed to replace the voices in my head with creativity and happiness, not with, "This is what you should do." And yes, I stayed in touch with this beautiful soul who was in pain, but I set the necessary boundaries to protect my own light.

When I finally moved to a new city, we had *both* grown.

Before I moved, he gave me a beautiful carved box with a card stuck to the inside that said, "You are always loved." He had found the strength to put on his own oxygen mask and get help. I had found wonderful work opportunities due to my renewed energy to create. And soon, he would come across one of the biggest opportunities of his own life, having found his way into more of the light himself.

To this day, we are friends. We both found love and happiness and have celebrated each other's lives. I cherish the moments we have had over the years to visit and catch up, despite the distance. And I kept that box until the day it practically disintegrated in my hands, worn and cracked and well used, a constant reminder that, yes, I am always loved and therefore worthy of looking after myself even if it meant having to pull away from someone else. Because, ultimately, I was of *more* service when I was my fullest, well-cared-for, Fun Size self.

There's a universal truth I knew in my head but still had to learn the hard way: You can't take care of anyone else if you haven't met your basic needs first. "Yes, yes, Anjali, I know, but there are so many people who depend on me and the urgent tasks I have to get done. I really can't stop and have a spa day right now."

Right, I hear you. And I agree. Sometimes what's urgent has to come first. There will be times when you have to sacrifice some (or a lot) of your own desires, energy, or resources for something or someone else. But that's not what I'm talking about here.

The words "self-care" get thrown around like hotcakes these days, and it's hard to really know what they mean. I've spent decades figuring out what enables me to function at my best. And I'm not always great at it. If I'm being completely honest, it used to take a lot of work and focus for me to remember to do some of the most basic things for myself before I tried to take care of everyone else around me.

I used to say with alarming regularity, "I feel like I need to go to human being camp." I was really good at what seemed like very complex activities, but when it came to understanding my basic needs, I was clueless. I depended on others to tell me what I "should" do, which only confused me more. There's a whole industry of advertisers and magazines built on telling us what to do and how to achieve this illustrious self-care nirvana (with their product, of course). But who's right? Who do I listen to?

Also, when I *did* decide to prioritize something I felt I needed over what someone else wanted, I would feel guilty or selfish. I would think, *I can take care of myself later. It's okay, I don't need that full night's sleep/quiet time/workout/healthy meal/(insert important self-care taking activity that I really shouldn't be ignoring here).*

The slippery slope of ignoring those basics is that it becomes easier and easier to "move the goalposts", as they say. What feels like a tiny compromise in self-care can lead to larger ones. It may have started with letting tiny things slide, then suddenly, I was compromising activities that were important to reaching goals that mattered to me. I was making work decisions—life decisions—based on what others wanted from me rather than what I knew I *needed*. I was running around passing out free oxygen masks on the brink of unconsciousness myself.

This isn't a new concept. I'm not the first to say these words. But just remember, as you're racing through your day, whether as a student cramming for finals or a parent juggling kids and a full-time job, when you are flying Fun Size Airlines, it's critical to make sure your oxygen mask is secure *first*. Basics like good nutrition, sleep, fresh air, exercise, solitude, self-compassion, and yes, even play, are the foundation of being able to take care of all the rest.

It's not optional, kids. If you're spending hours on the phone helping friends with their struggles, do you have somewhere or someone with whom you're able to work through your own? While you're racing around helping others with their challenges, are you giving yourself time to read, de-stress, be quiet and grateful, and revel in happiness? You want to be more productive, more successful, more loving and loved? Take really good care of the person you are and the body you're in. We only have one of you in the whole Universe, and we need you happy and well. Get that oxygen mask on and breathe in. *Then* you can be ready to be of service to those around you. Please take care of yourself. You have a lot of good to do.

CHARLEY LESSON #4: IT'S TIME FOR CHARLEYBAAAAAALLLLLLLLLL!

Like most dogs (and, frankly, a lot of people), little Charley Boo is easily wooed by one thing: food. The promise of a T-R-E-A-T will get him to do just about anything. He's an Olympic-caliber high jumper when I've got some noms in my hand, and while he won't beg, he will certainly stare at us longingly whenever we are eating just about anything. (Except kale. He will straight up walk *around* a piece of kale if it drops on the floor. I mean, do you blame him?)

Charley also has such a love for food that he will practically inhale anything that is put in front of him to eat. So in an effort to keep him from swallowing his meals whole, long ago, I purchased a small kibble ball that slows him down as he eats his meal. It's one of the most adorable things to watch him kick it around like a professional soccer player, and during the pandemic, he found another way to make it even more fun: He won't even play unless I'm playing with him. And you know if *I'm* playing, we're gonna make it a full-on *game*. Here's how it goes:

Every morning, the kibble ball gets filled up, and Charley moves into his starting position at the edge of the living room carpet. I loudly announce, "It's time for... CHARLEYBAAAAAAAALLLLLL!" and squat down to his level, holding the magical ball in my hands. Then—the standoff. Charley looks about 45 degrees to my left, I look to my right, and we freeze until one of us breaks and the game begins. From there, my commentary continues as Charley and I chase each other and the ball around the room until he's eaten all the food.

Yes. Yes, I am the crazy dog lady. You know what else? This dog reminds me every day that there are ways to make every challenge a game, even if it's just the challenge of keeping your dog from sucking down his entire meal in two seconds flat. When the challenges of this middle part of the journey catch you taking things too seriously, Charley (or any dog) will remind you that anything can be a game if you let it. And how can you keep from smiling when you're lookin' at that furry little face?

IS IT REJECTION OR PROJECTION?

People ask me all the time, "How do you deal with rejection?" as if, because I'm an actor, I must be good at handling rejection. After all, so much of what we do as actors involves rejection, right? The endless auditions, the disappointments, the public and private scrutiny. "It must be so hard. How do you possibly handle being rejected all the time?"

My answer used to vary from, "I don't," to "Not well," to "I just do."

I realize those are very different answers, but the one thing they have in common is that they reveal I don't have some tried and true method of feeling good or even okay about being rejected. Feeling rejected sucks. Of *course* it sucks. And anyone who tells you it doesn't or it's fine is, in my opinion, either lying to themselves or to you.

Does it mean you can't do anything to move past it? Of course not. But if I denied that I hate it and that it hurts, it would be like denying that touching a hot pot burns. That said, if someone asked me, "Oh my gosh, you cook so much. How do you deal with getting burned?" I would likely say the same thing: "I just do."

I suppose a lot of it boils down to just dealing with it. Not "accepting" it but doing what it takes to keep going. Doing the needful. That's really what I think of most unwanted emotions. Do I *want* to feel grief? No, of course not. But to pretend I don't feel it would be a lie. To try to sweep it away or push it off would also deny me a huge and vital part of my life experience. How do I deal with it? I just put one foot in front of the other and go moment to moment. I just. Keep. Going.

However, here is one whopper of a tool that can make getting past rejection a lot faster: Ask yourself if it's actually *rejection* at all.

As an actor, there may be 10/100/1,000 people auditioning for one role. So it stands to reason that only *one* of those people will be chosen for the role. Does that mean that the other 9/99/999 people all suck and should give up acting? No. Those people just weren't picked. Still, we often take the disappointment we feel in not being chosen and turn that disappointment inward. We make it so personal and hurtful by turning a "no" into a personal rejection.

After hearing "no" as many times as I have—including times I so desperately wanted to hear "yes"—I have realized disappointment *does not* equal rejection. That pain of disappointment does not have to turn into a referendum on your worth as a person. It's these times when it's vital to have a good, loving conversation with yourself. And since so often when we are hurting we revert to that tiny child inside who just wants to be loved, it's helpful to talk to yourself like you would talk to that little one.

Okay, Anj, I might say, *this really sucks. And it hurts. You wanted this so badly, and I know how much it stings.*

It does. I mean, what the fuck? (Wow, this kid has a mouth on her.) *What's wrong with me that they don't want me?*

Nothing's 'wrong' with you, you just weren't the one they chose this time. For this thing.

But I wanted this one so badly.

I know, sweetheart. But something else will come along that you want just as badly and you'll get it. I know that doesn't help right now, though.

It really doesn't.

I know you're disappointed. What would make you feel better?

Now, you're focused on feeling the disappointment and moving through it rather than catching it like a football and running it into the wrong end zone.

Feel your feelings. Identify what they really are. Don't turn them into a narrative about your worthiness or how loveable you are. Someone else saying "no" is *not* an indication of your worthiness or lovability. When you're experiencing disappointment, try to remind yourself what a loving, talented, powerful person you are. And until you have the space to evaluate what happened and learn from it (if there are lessons to be learned), find something that might make you feel better. I find 19 times out of 10, snuggling with a dog works for me. Charley gives great hugs.

KNOWING YOUR WORTH

It was a bittersweet moment of victory. No, not victory, but at least of dipping my toe back into the pool of my own self-worth. I was still shaking my head trying to understand the words that had been said to me by this person who ostensibly loved me. I and my boyfriend at the time—let's call him Danny—who I had been on-again-off again dating for several years, were having a heated conversation about, of all things, vocal production for stage actors (such a seemingly unemotional, theatre geek topic, I know) when he said the words, "Well, I can't expect you to know what you're talking about, you didn't go to grad school."

I had to literally repeat what I heard him say out loud and back to him to confirm that I had heard correctly. And when Danny confirmed that he had indeed said it, in a daze I just said, "Okay, I have to go." He made some kind of comment like, "Come on don't be like that," but I was too busy being utterly confused. We were both actors, and I was having great success and joy in the work I was doing, yet this person who loved me was saying I didn't know what I was talking about after singing in musicals my whole artistic life and all my studies through the years.

But truly, that wasn't what was throwing me for such a loop. The hardest aspect of that moment was realizing that a part of me was thinking, *Well, he's probably right. I mean, just because you have made a living doing this for so many years doesn't mean you know what you're doing.*

He's so confident, maybe he does know so much more than you do and you don't know anything.

And then thankfully, this more pertinent thought came up in my head: *If I stay with someone who doesn't respect me or my intelligence, what am I saying to myself? And what have I been saying to myself this whole time? Because this really isn't the first time this has happened.* It wasn't the first time. Not by far.

I remember when I used to think so many people in my life were hell-bent on criticizing me or making me feel badly about things. To be fair, some of them were. But I think that's also because there was a long period in my life where—for whatever reason—I seemed to trust the harsh and critical voices more than those who were loving and supportive.

If a teacher told me I was a natural or gifted, I would thank them and barely take it in, but I would hold on to the voice of the teacher who told me that I wasn't really good enough or didn't have the natural talent needed to make it. More embarrassing to admit, I felt that way in romantic relationships, too. If a guy was consistently kind and complimentary, I would blow it off as him just trying to make me feel good or having ulterior motives, but if I went out with someone who was confident to the point of arrogance and led with suggestions on how to improve myself/my career/my finances/my life, I was smitten. *I mean, this person* must *know more than I do, right? I'm such a mess, and they're so confident. I'm sure they have all the answers. I should listen to this great guru of all things because they obviously can solve all my problems.*

In *The Four Agreements: A Practical Guide to Personal Freedom*,[5] Don Miguel Ruiz talks about one of the reasons we allow others to treat us poorly:

> "The way we judge ourselves is the worst judge that ever existed. If we make a mistake in front of people, we try to deny the mistake and cover it up. But as soon as we are alone, the Judge becomes so strong, the guilt is so strong, and we feel so stupid, or so bad, or so unworthy. In your whole life nobody has ever abused you more than you have abused yourself. And the limit of your self-abuse is exactly the limit that you will tolerate from someone else. If someone abuses you a little more than you abuse yourself, you will probably walk away from that person. But if someone abuses you a little less than you abuse yourself, you will probably stay in the relationship and tolerate it endlessly. Why? Because in your belief system you say, 'I deserve it. This person is doing me a favor by being with me. I'm not worthy of love and respect. I'm not good enough.'"

I look back at those times, the people I surrounded myself with and listened to, and worse, the people who loved me who I *wasn't* listening to, and I feel so badly for that young woman. She didn't have a sense of her own worth. It took hitting rock bottom—actually, several rock bottoms—

before I started listening to the voice inside me that I had pushed down for too long. She was still in there, but just like my loved ones and dear friends who *were* supportive and encouraging, I had blown her off for so long I could barely hear her. She was saying, *You're worth more than this. I don't care how much of a screwup you are, and really you're not so bad, but even if you were, you are worthy of more than this.*

To add insult to injury, when I did have any kind of success or progress in my life, I wouldn't allow myself to take credit for any of it. When I moved up from being an understudy to being the lead of a huge Broadway show, I tempered the joy by telling myself, *It's just because I fit the costume* (which was utterly ridiculous since plenty of people fit the costume, and there was a whole costume crew there ready to make needed alterations). When I booked any television job that involved medical jargon, I would say, *It's just because both my parents are doctors.* Never mind that I still had to learn the lines, the blocking, and, ya know, *act.*

When an incredibly lovely British man took me out to one of the nicest dinners I'd had in my time in New York up until then and treated me like a princess, I told myself, *Oh it's just because I'm Indian, and I know he loves Indian culture.* Never mind that this sweet man, who happened to be well-traveled, actually had a respect for and interest in who I was outside of my background, and we spent more of our time talking about theatre and life and love than anything about India.

I realize now the problem wasn't with the negative voices inside and outside of me. The problem was that *I was listening to them*. Not just listening, but hanging on their every word, allowing my own opinion of myself and my worthiness to depend on their judgment, their assessment, their lack of love.

There was a strange if/then understanding that I had created. The harder someone was to please, the more their favor meant because it was so hard to get. If that handsome but wildly arrogant guy wanted to be with me, then it must mean I was special because he told me all the time he could be with anyone else. If that teacher who directed so many shows outside of school told me I did a good job today, then it must mean it's true because most of the time, he's just telling me what's wrong with me and why I won't make it as an actress.

In reality, the only person whose opinion mattered, the one person who had the power not just to make me happy but truly successful in all aspects of my life, was *me*. But I didn't deem myself worthy of love, so I was looking for outside approval to prove myself wrong. I wasn't confident I deserved a great career, so I was dependent on teachers and directors and casting directors to tell me I was capable. I wasn't giving myself that one basic foundational gift we all need to be able to thrive: Knowing. My. Worth.

The harsh truth here is that I didn't want to take credit for my success or happiness because then I had to take responsibility for it. And I didn't know how on Earth to create either consistently enough to trust that I would feel worthy because of my own actions. What I didn't realize then, and what I'm hoping you can see for yourself now, is that worthiness doesn't come from outside of you or even from the things you create for yourself. It is something that comes innately from you. It is the basic act of valuing yourself, allowing yourself to see that you are important to the people around you, to the world, that you have so much to offer just by being precisely who you are. And that the world would be a sadder place without you because you are the only you we have.

Knowing your worth means knowing you have value beyond your accomplishments, beyond your relationship status, beyond the money you have in your bank, the followers you have on your accounts, the items you own, the things you surround yourself with. Your value comes from the unique set of traits and eccentricities and thoughts and experiences that make you *you*. And yes, it means you are responsible for your own happiness—but the great joy of that is that it means you always have the power to create that happiness for yourself. Yes, Spider-Man, with great power comes great responsibility, but with great responsibility comes great power. And *that* power, the power that comes from knowing you are worthy and valuable and in charge of your own happiness is incredibly fun to wield.

THE WORLD WOULD BE A SADDER PLACE WITHOUT YOU BECAUSE YOU ARE THE ONLY YOU WE HAVE.

Listen to that voice inside you that reminds you how valuable and worthy you are, even if you can barely hear it right now. Dial into that frequency and focus on it—hard. That's the voice to trust, to follow, to amplify, and to listen to every chance you get.

Part 2: The Messy Middle

CARA THEOBOLD
ACTRESS (DOWNTON ABBEY, ABSENTIA, READY PLAYER ONE, CRAZYHEAD), VOICE ACTRESS (OVERWATCH), ALL-AROUND SWEETHEART
WWW.IAMFUNSIZE.COM/CARATHEOBOLD

"Don't care what people think about you. Go for it. Do what you want to do. Go for your dreams, and don't worry about pleasing other people. Also: For anyone of any age, always eat the French toast."

A Space Opera Trilogy (Sort Of)

"Make an empty space in any corner of your mind, and creativity will fill in." – Dee Hock

MAKING SPACE

It was my senior year of college. I was in acting class with that same acting teacher of mine, Mary Poole (yes, I have *two* brilliant Marys in my life; I am very Mary-blessed), and the question was something to the effect of, "What do you think you could most improve on as an actor?" Everyone was coming up with brilliant, incisive answers, and I felt the pressure mounting as it came closer and closer to my turn. I was terrified because for the life of me I couldn't focus on the question. I was thinking of so many different things at once: the next class, the rehearsal I had after class, the homework I had to do for this class, the date I was supposed to go on after rehearsal, all the things I had to do...

"Anjali?"

I took a deep breath, and then, pure honesty.

"I honestly have no idea right now because my brain is so full I can't even see straight."

Forget about insight, talent, creativity, inspiration. There was no room in my hard drive to process the data that was already there. It was like there was a spinning circle of death (Mac users, you know the one) and the error message, "Your disk is full. You must delete files before continuing." (Little did I know that was the perfect answer because right there was the number one block in my acting work and creativity in general.)

I wish I could say that was the turning point for me, that I somehow had an aha moment right then and there at the young age of 21. But no, this is a situation I've found myself in time and time again. Overfilled, but not in that beautiful "my cup runneth over" way, more in that "spinning circle of death" way.

Months later, the movie *Contact* came out and my boyfriend, Gregg, and I went to see it. I'll skip over all the beautiful things I loved about that movie (man, I need to go back and watch it again) and head right to the part that had me saying, *Okay, Universe, I'm hearing this*. It was Jodie Foster's monologue at the end during her final hearing. I have no idea what she said. It wasn't about the words. Something about her delivery—about *her*—struck me in the heart. It felt like she was a vessel, letting something greater than herself run through her. I had the mental image of water flowing from the Universe through her and out to us.

I tried to explain it to Gregg afterwards but eventually told him I needed to go home and process before I could even talk about the movie. I'd had this somewhat spiritual experience, but it wasn't even about the movie. It was about the importance of making space inside me to allow inspiration to flow through. To free up memory and disk space on my hard drive. To make the space to think. To create. To feel. To be.

In recent years, as the world has become more and more complicated, I'm realizing how imperative it is that we protect the space inside us and leave a little bit of it free to dream and process the input we get from the outside world. Not just the obvious input like things we may be studying, but all the conversations, sounds, sights, feelings, sensations, music, you name it. Even without our gadgets, without company, the world today is so full of noise, it is up to us to make the space to *think* and *create* and *feel* and *be*.

It is vital that we build some space into our world—solitude, quiet, without books, without gadgets, without TV, without conversation—to let our magical, magnificent brains process all they take in. Create some space in your schedule for simply thinking and being. And don't make the sneaky mistake (that I absolutely have done) of turning it into a productivity exercise. Just let it be processing time.

We understand that our computers need this, so if you have to imagine yourself as a computer, do it. Turn on your own personal disk repair app in your head. (I find hiking to be a magnificent way to do this.) Doing something physical where your body is working but not so hard that you need to focus on what it's doing. Long distance drives are great for this, too, provided you aren't texting—insert judgmental auntie face staring at you if you are—or listening to the radio or podcasts at the same time. Throw the phone in your bag or the back seat if that's what it takes to create some space on your long drive. And see what comes up in your mind.

> **IT IS VITAL WE BUILD SOME SPACE INTO OUR WORLD— SOLITUDE AND QUIET, WITHOUT BOOKS, GADGETS, TV, OR CONVERSATION—TO LET OUR MAGICAL, MAGNIFICENT BRAINS PROCESS ALL THEY TAKE IN.**

One way to do this at home (although, warning, it often looks to others like you're doing "nothing," and they'll want to interrupt you, so try to do this in private!) is to get some paper and pencil or pen. (Don't use your phone notes; go old school with me.) Stare into space for a moment. If you can, find a blank wall so there is really no input coming at you through your field of vision. With your eyes open, breathe. If thoughts of to-dos and discomfort and wanting to grab your phone or your laptop start to jump in, take another breath and guide your focus back to the blank space. Focus on the feeling of your breath, just breathing in and out however is comfortable to you. If you have to, write down any urgent matters that pop into your head.

After about two minutes of staring at this wall or soft focus into space, see what pops into your head that isn't go, go, go. Are there questions that come up? Write them down. Ideas? Inspirations? Write those down. Maybe ask the Universe for a little help. Ask yourself, "Is there anything deeply on my mind today?" See if anything outside of your normal set of thoughts comes up. I find resetting like this throughout my day can give me space in an otherwise overwhelming day.

Also, there are some wonderful books on the importance of focus and creating space in your life. One of my favorites in recent years is a book I already mentioned: *Essentialism* by Greg McKeown. Also check out *Deep Work: Rules for Focused Success in a Distracted World* and *Digital Minimalism: Choosing a Focused Life in a Noisy World* by Cal Newport. And for a quick and very personal read on the topic, check out my friend Samantha Joy's book, *The Less Effect: Design Your Life for Happiness & Purpose*.

TAKING SPACE

Growing up, I noticed there was a funny thing that seemed to happen with people of diminutive size. In my experience, people went one of two ways: they (particularly women) either bought into other people's assessment of their stature and continued that narrative by speaking quietly and leaning into "cute" and "quiet" and "sweet," or they went 180 degrees in the other direction, almost in defiance of what the outer perception of them was. The folks on this end would speak as loudly as they could to make sure they were heard and their presence was known in every room, and they'd be the first one to help people pick up heavy things, basically letting the world know that whether or not they could *see* it on the outside, this person was a force to be reckoned with on the inside.

I'll give you one guess which one I was—and still am, to

some degree. I mean, I just wrapped a TV show where, at the wrap party, they gave out gag awards to the cast and creative team and mine was "Most Likely to Be Heard Before She Is Seen," to which all I could reply was, "Yeah, that tracks."

That said, there have been plenty of times in my life where I *felt* small, where I could feel my fear or anxiety or just general lack of confidence causing me to withdraw further into myself instead of expanding. Instead of being Fun Size in the way I use it in this book, I was doing everything I could to disappear.

I remember feeling so indignant when I heard from a boyfriend once, "It just feels like the better I am, the smaller you get." Yeeeeowwwch. Never mind that this guy (who I now know was a dyed-in-the-wool narcissist) didn't quite understand that what was making him feel better was constantly undermining me, it still felt like a true assessment. I *was* feeling smaller and smaller and less myself the more I allowed myself to take in those unkind words or believe in the negative assessments being made of me.

Napoleon complexes aside, though, there is something wonderful about being willing to own not only the space you take up, but *taking up the space you choose to own*. This same phenomenon, interestingly enough, applies to many people of much taller stature. I've seen so many beautifully statuesque women (and some men) doing everything they can to seem smaller, take up less space, almost apologizing for the wondrous body they inhabit and how much room it takes up.

> **THERE IS SOMETHING WONDERFUL ABOUT BEING WILLING TO OWN NOT ONLY THE SPACE YOU TAKE UP, BUT TAKING UP THE SPACE YOU CHOOSE TO OWN.**

Mind you, let me be very clear: This is *not* an argument for manspreading. Or womanspreading. Or anyone spreading. Taking up the space, *owning* the space around you is an energetic thing. Whether someone is loud or quiet, tall or small, or any shape at all, the space they own is something that speaks volumes about their comfort in their own skin. Remember, these bodies are just vehicles for our souls, and the energy that those souls can emit is unlimited. That energy is not only important for our own confidence, it's important for the *world*.

Have you ever been in a room where someone walks in, and without them saying a word, you *feel* the grounding, the warmth, or ooooh best of all, the love coming off them? There is incredible power in your presence, in the vibrational energy of authenticity, of self-ownership, of knowing who you are, and by God, it's not just your right to know it, it's your *responsibility*. There is only one of you in the whole world, and without the contribution of your unique energy signature, we all lose something special.

It can be very easy to let the ravages of disappointment, grief, or sadly, other people's cruel words to somehow diminish that light, that vibration, that energy. You've read about my experiences in relationships, like the one above, where the words I heard and the behavior I both saw and allowed made me feel smaller and smaller each day. But it is up to you, dear, dear reader, not to let that happen to you. There is nothing good in the world that makes you feel *less* than your biggest, fullest, Fun Size self. Own your space, take it for yourself. And don't let anyone take it from you. It's not theirs to have, it's yours to own.

HOLDING SPACE

Years ago, during one of the first times we were spending quality time together, I listened as one of my now best friends in all the world told me about a particularly difficult time she was going through, how she was having trouble finding hope in the moment. I remember saying to her, "I see it all for you. You don't have to see it right now; you just be where you are and be good to yourself. But I'm telling you, I'm here holding space for all of what's to come because you have no idea how amazing you are." And over the course of the next few years, as she found her footing and her way back to herself, I watched her step into even more of her beauty and greatness than she had before.

While her gratitude for my support during that time means so much to me, what really means the most is the joy I get from knowing she made this happen *all by herself*. All I did was be one person who believed without fail that she would not only survive this tough period, but she would thrive and make magic out of it that she didn't even know was possible.

ANJALI BHIMANI

One of the greatest gifts you can give someone—including yourself—is to hold space within you for the possibility of, well, anything. Anything at all. To be willing to imagine a world where what may *seem* impossible is possible. Although it's usually much easier for us to do this for other people, that doesn't mean it's too hard to do for yourself. It just means you might need a little more practice at it.

There have been so many times in my life when I've heard a friend or loved one lamenting a situation, and in my own head and heart, I see them—their radiant, kind, talented, hilarious self—and realize they can't see how incredible they are. Perhaps a relationship or a circumstance or maybe just getting up on the wrong side of the bed was somehow clouding their future vision so much, they couldn't possibly see something changing. I've found this most often with people in their relationships: a friend who's had his heart broken, or a loved one who has a seemingly terrible relationship with her family member, or a relationship of my own where one person is trying to change something big within themselves but the people around them haven't allowed for the possibility that they could make such a drastic shift.

I have to admit, I find it wildly exciting to hold space for people in my life who are healing from something or struggling with something because I get to see what greatness will come when they bust through the moment of pain or frustration or anger they are in. It's not something you tell people you're doing. It's just something you do. In my head, quietly, it looks like this: *I know this is what's happening now. I know you're hurting, and I'm so sorry. I wish you weren't in pain right now. You might not be able to see what's possible, but I'm holding a space for you to be so happy/fulfilled/loved/proud of yourself you will look back on this time and see precisely why this moment needed to happen to get you there. And when you are there, oh* man *will we celebrate.*

ONE OF THE GREATEST GIFTS YOU CAN GIVE SOMEONE—INCLUDING YOURSELF—IS TO HOLD SPACE WITHIN YOU FOR THE POSSIBILITY OF, WELL, ANYTHING.

Again, I don't always say that out loud to them. People can't be yanked out of their pain. Nor should they be. It can royally piss someone off when they are hurting to tell them you see how amazing their life is going to be. As I've said before, we all need the freedom to feel what we are feeling in the moment. But having that mindset, silently holding that space for those in pain, is glorious. *And you can do it for yourself, too.*

Look, we live in a world where the impossible has been proven possible over and over again. Cars, elevators, planes, rocket ships—science fiction has become just plain science because *someone* held the space for possibility. But without that belief in anything being possible, they couldn't have taken the steps toward creating it. And yes, sometimes that means leaning on people who believe in it for you when you can't do it for yourself—until that moment when you can.

ANJALI BHIMANI

MAKE SPACE TO THINK, TO BELIEVE, TO CREATE.

Part 2: The Messy Middle

Take Space to Radiate and Revel in Your Unique Energy and Power.

Anjali Bhimani

Hold space for anything to be possible.

Part 2: The Messy Middle

My Secret to Staying Positive All the Time

Maybe it's because of the videos I post, or my excitement when I am at conventions meeting new people, or my refusal to use social media for anything other than inspiring people, making people smile, bragging about my friends and their awesome accomplishments, and posting dog pictures, but I get asked a lot by the online community what my secret is to staying upbeat, positive, and optimistic all the time. The first time I read that question in my inbox, my knee-jerk reaction was to snort-laugh and end up with coffee up my nose. *If only they knew what happens behind the scenes...*

So, you ready for the big secret? Here ya go...drum roll....

I don't stay positive all the time. Not. Even. Close. And frankly, sometimes I actually court a little bit of negativity.

Look, we're all human. Whatever greater power is out there, whether it's God or Buddha or cheddar cheese, it gave us these beautiful bodies to drive around the planet and house our souls, and those souls and bodies have *feelings*. They're not morally good or bad; they just are. I'm not here to tell myself or anyone else not to feel them. In fact, I've been known to get into arguments with someone (aka my husband) just to be allowed to feel like crap about something because I *want* to feel something and move through it and past it on my own terms. I'm all about the whole experience.

Maybe there are more evolved beings out there (well, not maybe; I'm pretty sure of it because the goofy snort-laugh that sometimes comes out of me is *not* the sound of a highly evolved being), but I doubt even they would say being positive all the time is a great move. It can blind you to things you might actually need to see. In fact, "toxic positivity" is a phrase we've started to hear more and more in our world because sometimes things *are* bad. And we need to be able to see them for what they are in order to solve them.

We all have our moments. I snap, I cry, I whine, I catch myself saying ridiculous things out loud or in my head when I'm in a bad mood. I'm just grateful there isn't a camera on me 24-7, and that the people I'm closest to who have to see it are incredibly understanding humans who know who I am at my core and will lovingly let me have my meltdown or tell me to snap out of it. (My husband has earned his doctorate in "speaking Anjali," and there are days that man should be up for sainthood. Truly. Along with my mom and my best friends.)

Some of the greatest creations of all time have come from a series of very much *not* positive feelings, including the righteous indignation of an injustice or the pain and sadness that comes from compassion for another person's plight. Compassionate anger can be a tremendous creative force, whether it inspires someone to right a social injustice or just to create a product or service for an underserved portion of the population.

In *Die Empty: Unleash Your Best Work Every Day*, Todd Henry explains, "My personal mission is driven primarily by the compassionate anger I feel on behalf of overworked professionals."[6] My own frustrations with some of the battles I have fought with myself and my desperate desire to keep others from going through the same thing is largely the inspiration for the *I Am Fun Size* series and this book.

So yeah, my personal way to handle negativity? Release the pressure on yourself to always be positive. Give yourself permission to feel like crap for a second. Positive is not the only goal. Energized, creative, driven, useful—those are things to aim for. And that last one is the one that probably drives me the most to move efficiently and thoroughly through difficult emotions and painful thoughts because I know what I learn might be useful to someone else (not to mention I'm not so useful to the world when I'm curled up in a ball under the covers).

Also, at least one really good snort-laugh a day is a pretty good way to fend off negativity. Belly laughs are even better. I find having an adorable dog around is an excellent way to make sure this happens on the reg. (I mean, have you been *seeing* these pics of Charley? Again, @charleythebestdog on IG. Just sayin'.)

THOUGHTS ON LONELINESS

Each week, people from all over the world send in questions for me and my friends to answer in an *I Am Fun Size* episode. This was one of my favorite questions to answer of the whole series so far because my answer took me by surprise as well: "What is loneliness? Why do we feel lonely? Why is it that I can be in a room full of people and feel so alone?"

It's such a simple question, but I knew—both from my own experience and from talking to so many who have felt the same way over the years—it required more than just a simple answer. Being someone who loves her alone time, there has been so clear a difference between the feeling of loneliness and being alone. So when I sat quietly, closed my eyes, and meditated on those times when I felt the loneliest, that little voice in my head served up these words: *I've felt the loneliest in my life when I'm not enjoying my own company.*

Well now, that hit me right between the eyes. Simultaneously so simple and yet such a tricky thing to do when you're feeling low. And what does that even mean? To enjoy your own company?

In my experience, the times that I have felt the loneliest are not just the times that I feel disconnected from other people. Sure, as human beings we innately need to feel connected to other people. We want to bond, and we're not the only species who does. We see it all over nature; physical connection is vital to our well-being. But circumstances of 2020 (and beyond) aside, loneliness can extend far beyond when we are physically alone.

Looking back, I can see that I spent a good chunk of my life looking for almost anyone outside of myself to help me not feel lonely, to help me feel like I belong, like I was connected. I turned to everyone else for confirmation that I mattered and that I was worth loving. And when I was alone, the unkind thoughts about myself would grow louder and louder.

When I was alone as a kid, I was creative. I would make construction paper animals. I would draw my Dungeons and Dragons characters and write stories about them. I would create forts and obstacle courses for my hamster and dance around my room.

But at some point in my life, that changed. I began to notice that when I was alone, I spoke to myself in extremely unkind ways. Criticizing myself, telling myself that I wasn't good enough, that I would never find a boyfriend because I wasn't pretty or popular or talented or successful enough — truly unkind things I would never say to anyone else, yet here I was saying those things on a loop to the person I spent the most time with—me. What I realized after a time was that I felt lonely because I was looking for someone else to drown out the voice in my own head that I so didn't want to hear. I wasn't enjoying my own company.

Now the flip side of that isn't that I had to run around telling myself how great I was, but I definitely *did* have to learn to speak to myself like someone I actually wanted to be around. To replace the old recordings in my head with newer, more interesting and supportive thoughts. To be someone I wanted to be around even in my own mind. Someone who had interesting conversations to share, not hurtful words that made me feel small. Someone who had a great sense of humor, not someone so dour and angry who only saw my failings. I wouldn't want to be with someone who treated me the way I was treating myself. So how could I possibly expect to enjoy being alone if I was treating myself so poorly?

Changing those tapes, re-recording them, and playing them back can take a little time (and honestly, that was an actual tool I used—recording myself saying different words or even listening to audiobooks and speaking them out loud as I was listening to drown out that cruel voice in my mind), but it is such an important thing to do for yourself. Be the person to yourself that you want to find outside of you, the person you want to hang out with, to share deep thoughts with, to have a good snort laugh with. Be kind and make yourself laugh. Treat yourself to exploring new places and new experiences. Read and sing to yourself. Be compassionate to yourself in moments of weakness or failure. Be the person you want to be around. And see if maybe the next time you're feeling lonely, you can tap into that partner-in-crime within yourself and enjoy the ride together.

WHO'S IN YOUR HEAD?

It was my senior year of college when I should ostensibly be preparing to take my acting skills out into the "real" world, and I was starting to get wildly discouraged about my ability to make acting my profession. I had just finished doing the rounds of auditions for that quarter's shows and hadn't landed a role. Again. I asked one of my professors for help, for feedback. *What was I doing wrong?* His incredibly useful (note heavy sarcasm here) input was: "Well, you sing okay, you dance okay, I haven't seen you act but I'm sure you're fine, but you don't do anything really well." He then followed up by saying, "It's not just because of your background, but you should look into musicals like *Flower Drum Song*, *Miss Saigon*, and *West Side Story*." Ummmm. The only thing I could see at the time that those three musicals had in common is that they have leading roles that aren't Caucasian.

Why is it that despite all the support and encouragement I got from so many of my professors, *this* is one of my top five memories from my time in acting school? I *know* there was positive reinforcement for so many of my performances. I remember hearing it. I just don't remember who said it or what was said. But those words above? Etched in my memory like a carving in stone.

The same goes for relationships. For years, no matter who told me how much they loved me, the words that stuck were the hurtful ones. So much so that I remember being in rehearsal with Mary Z. and making some harsh comment about myself, and she looked at me and said, "Anjali, I wish you would just see yourself the way we see you. You're just so great and talented and beautiful." The kindness of that simple statement was so profound and yet so saddening because I recognized how hard it was for me to actually hold onto those kind words most of the time. I was letting the hurtful ones take up too much space in my head. And worse, it was so obvious to someone outside me that I loved so much that she felt she needed to tell me right then and there, perhaps so I could hear the people around us agree with her. It was such an act of love on her part, and one of many wake-up calls for me to stop that brutal voice in my head because it was starting to come out my mouth. A lot.

Have you ever heard the statement, "You are the sum of the five people you spend the most time with"? It's a popular maxim to remind us to be around people who believe in us, inspire us, make us feel good and laugh, and allow us to be the biggest self we can be. I'd like to take that statement a step further. It's not just the top five people around you who shape the kind of person you are; it's also the top five voices in your head that shape who you *believe* yourself to be.

Whose words are you taking in at the moment? Whose words are you letting live in that premium space in your head and heart? Is it the best friend who knows you inside and out and loves you and supports you and roots for your success? Or are you ignoring them and just listening to that *one* person online who said something awful and you can't get them out of your head?

Are you paying attention to the boss or professor who lauded your talent or are you still aching from the wound of the interviewer who said you were unqualified or somehow unworthy? Are you listening to the new guy or girl in your life who loves spending time with you and makes you feel special or are you still holding on to the words of that ex (or, God forbid, current partner) telling you you're less than, not pretty enough, not tall enough, or whatever?

Most of all, who are *you* being in your head? Which voice are you using? Are you compassionate and kind to yourself or are you curt, unforgiving, and rude? Are you the voice of encouragement or the voice of negative reinforcement? You are the only person who spends 24 hours a day, 7 days a week with yourself, so of all the people in your life, you need to make sure you are being the best person to yourself and for yourself. It's not just a trope. If you wouldn't spend time with someone who is cruel to you in the outside world, why would you want to spend time with that person inside your own head?

Make sure that while you're choosing friends and partners and colleagues, you're being extra picky about who gets to take up your mental real estate. Your brain is your most powerful asset, and the people who sit in the front row of that glorious mental theatre of yours better deserve those premium seats.

PART 2: THE MESSY MIDDLE

IF YOU WOULDN'T SPEND TIME WITH SOMEONE WHO IS CRUEL TO YOU IN THE OUTSIDE WORLD, WHY WOULD YOU WANT TO SPEND TIME WITH THAT PERSON INSIDE YOUR OWN HEAD?

CHARLEY LESSON #5: YOU KNOW WHAT WOULD MAKE US BOTH FEEL BETTER?

It was the first time the little guy had ever seen me cry (or at least that's how I remember it): I was sitting on the bed in my room in the apartment I shared with arguably one of the most high-energy and adventurous human beings I've ever known (Liz Del Sol, I'm talkin' about you), and as I had only just recently moved in with her, I didn't feel so comfortable sharing my "tender underbelly" as it were. So I was sitting on the bed, back up against the wall, when Charley pushed his little nose through the door.

He hopped up on the bed, directly opposite from me, and cocked his head curiously.

Whatcha doin', Mama? You okay?

Then, he laid down on his belly and began to inch his way closer and closer to me. And looking me straight in the eye, he slowly rolled over on his back.

You know what would make us both feel better? If you give me a belly rub.

Immediately, I was laughing. This little compassionate nugget knew that the best way to get me out of whatever I was experiencing was to connect with his furry self, to step out of whatever was going on in my own head—I don't even remember what it was now, which just speaks to the power of Charley's snuggliciousness—and connect with another creature. And yes, to laugh.

Just another bit of wisdom from the furry fella: When in doubt, a little laugh and a little snuggle goes a long, long way. If you hit it jusssssst right, you might even forget what you were sad about in the first place.

MELANIE STONE
ACTRESS (MYTHICA, LITTLE WOMEN, WE'RE ALIVE: FRONTIER), ADVENTURER, AND EXCELLENT "LET'S MAKE UP A FUN SIZE DANCE" DANCE PARTNER
WWW.IAMFUNSIZE.COM/MELANIESTONE

"If we're not making an effort to be conscious about our choices, we can make tiny little steps that get away from who we are. If you have a tendency to people-please (like myself) you might do things to get approval or acceptance. Personally, I got to this point where I realized, 'Okay. This isn't me. Why am I doing this? I'm not happy, and I'm not making anybody else happy.' So it all came back to this: I need to be who I am, and screw it! If people don't like it, they don't like it. They can leave, and the people that do like your true self, they're the ones that you want in your life."

ARE YOU INSPIRING OR IN-SPIRAL-ING?

I was racing to my car in my sari, desperately trying to reach the safety of its confines before I erupted into tears. The audition, which I had been so hopeful about, had been a catastrophe. I was running late when I got there. There was a 10-minute walk from the parking lot to the building in the hot California sun, so when I arrived, I was out of breath and wilted. I had quickly composed myself in the bathroom before heading to the hallway where the actress who was before me, a stellar actress who I adore and who is incredibly accomplished, was just coming out, and I could hear the laughter and warmth emanating from the room after she left.

I walked into silence, except the casting director saying, "I'll be reading with you whenever you're ready." I began my scene, and within about 20 seconds of starting, one of the producers in the room casually picked up his phone and began—texting. I continued on but couldn't stop the voice in my head saying, *Oh my God, this guy is so bored and over you that he can't even wait two minutes to pick up his phone and text. There's no way you're getting this; you've blown it. They discounted you the second you walked in the room, probably because you look like such a mess after running in the heat. Everyone on the team is gonna be so disappointed you blew this one; it's such a great role,* and so on.

When I finally finished the scene, I got the perfunctory "thank you" from the casting director and immediately thought, *He's so disappointed. He's such a fan and you blew it. You're going to have to send him a message later. But first, get to the car before you lose your shit.*

The journey to the car was a blur because all I cared about was getting there before I fell apart. And when I did, sure enough, I just wept. I called my dear friend and manager, Caleigh Vancata, and left her a long message apologizing for blowing it and explaining that I thought I was prepared enough but somehow I must've not been that good, and on and on.

She called me back within minutes, and said, "So you wanna talk about it?" And the blubbering began anew. Amidst all the apologizing, the spiral continued until I finally hit a lull in my teary tirade. She took a breath and said, "Okay, are you done? Because you're the choice. They already called me. So take a breath, drink some water, and remember never to trust that voice in your head again."

We've all been there. We are driving to work, doing the dishes, or out on a run when we can't even enjoy the music or podcast or audiobook playing because we are too busy ruminating—or spiraling—about something we did or said. Or something someone else did or said.

It's fine, and totally normal, to have a negative thought or feeling, but I know I'm spiraling when, *Oof, you really blew that audition,* progresses into, *You embarrassed yourself. You had such a great chance in there and you really blew it. You think that casting director is going to call you in again? You should probably call your manager and apologize. And maybe see if she can tell the casting director you're sorry, too. You should never have quit acting classes, even if you needed a break; you don't deserve a break if you're doing work that is this bad. You should have prepared more, and now look what happened. You're so lazy, you're just such a failure,* and so on and so on. Suddenly, a perceived bad moment turns into a referendum on my personal character and worthiness as a human being.

It's easy to see how unhelpful and *untrue* that whole train of thought is when we read it, when we are on the outside of it. But let's face it, it's hard to decipher truth from lies when we are in our own head. We tend to talk to ourselves a lot harsher than we would if we were speaking out loud, and definitely than if we were speaking to someone else. And God forbid you *are* speaking to yourself out loud like this. That just feels even worse.

To help me pay attention to my own self-talk, especially the harsh kind, I love to use little catchphrases. I find them to be helpful in shutting down those pesky voices telling me things I really don't need to be listening to right now. And this one I owe to my dear friend, Ty Taylor, one of the most prolific artists I know (and incidentally, the person who introduced me to Rick when we both performed in a musical that Ty wrote years ago). He has a knack for dropping bits of brilliant wordplay in messages or quick phone calls just like he does in his beautiful songwriting. He gave me this term to use for an *I Am Fun Size* episode years ago, and here it is for you.

When I find myself spiraling, conflating all the things I perceive are and could be going wrong in my world, I take a moment to ask, *Anj, are you self-inspiring or self-*in-spiral-ing *right now? Are you allowing one thought that leads to another and another to take you down a desperate spiral of self-loathing or are you giving yourself some helpful feedback that gets you jazzed for the next chance to do better or grow or create something beautiful?*

For example, what if that same train of thought from before went like this:

> *Oof, I really blew that audition. Well, at least it feels like I did. And that's a huge bummer, doesn't feel good; I'm really disappointed with myself. I wonder what I can do right now to make myself feel better? I can wait for feedback, but I know that doesn't always come. I suppose I could have prepared more, but then again I did work with a coach and spent a good chunk of time on it, and I didn't want to over-rehearse, which is wise. Actually, come to think of it, they did laugh a lot while I was in the room, especially at that one joke. And they were really kind. I think I'm gonna write a thank you note to that casting director because*

they are such a lovely champion of actors, and it's always such a friendly room when I go in there. And I'm really looking forward to the next chance I get to go in.

Same disappointment to start, but by the end of that train of thought, I'm getting off at the station named, "I feel generous and thankful," rather than, "I feel unworthy and embarrassed." Which one of those stations feels like it's going to be the most productive one to land at? Yeah, I think so, too.

"Okay Anj, it's all very well and good not to be judgy and critical of myself, but let's face it, sometimes you really need to take a hard look at yourself and say you did something poorly/you're out of shape/you need to do better. I can't just tell myself I'm awesome at something when I know I could be better."

Oh, I couldn't agree with you more. In fact, I think trusting ourselves to be accurately critical is the only way we also really trust ourselves to know when we've done a good job. I mean, how many of us have blown off a compliment from our mom or loved one by saying, "Yeah but you always say that"? And we've all seen far too many examples of misguided parents on reality TV competitions telling their kids they're the next Christina Aguilera or John Legend when they can't hold a tune, followed by them being flabbergasted and wounded when the judges tell them they aren't moving on in the competition. We don't wanna be fooled, not even by ourselves, so how can we be accurate with our assessments without beating ourselves up and spiraling into a bottomless pit of doom and gloom?

> **FAILING AT SOMETHING DOESN'T MAKE YOU A FAILURE. IT JUST MEANS YOU FAILED—AND JUST THIS TIME. END OF STORY.**

It's the simple (but not easy) difference between judgment and evaluation. Yes, we need to assess ourselves and our accomplishments objectively to be able to improve things, of *course* we do. But when we assign a moral judgment to our level of accomplishment or failure, that's when things start to take a nasty detour. We go from inspiring ourselves to do better to convincing ourselves we *can't*. Even if I *had* truly stunk up the room on an audition, if I judged myself a loser as a *person* after that, what would be the chances of me trying to do better next time versus just giving up out of fear of failing again and again? Just like we wouldn't call a toddler stupid for falling a hundred times before they walk, we absolutely can't do that to ourselves when we are on the road to leading a big ol' Fun Size life. Failing at something doesn't make *you* a failure. It just means you failed—and just this time. End of story.

So, adventurers, inspire yourself as best you can, even in those moments when your own head might be telling you to spiral down. Diminishing your own light doesn't help anyone, but keeping it lit and full, even if it's flickering, can light the way for someone else, which is worth that train ticket to the right station every time.

PART 2: THE MESSY MIDDLE

FABULOUS FOMO

I could hear the sound of the birds in the tall, swaying trees just outside our lanai, and even from the bedroom inside, I could feel the gentle, warm breeze wafting in from outdoors. The cozy bed underneath me was so comfortable that sitting on it made me just want to curl up under the covers again if not for the fact that it was late in the morning, and I was so eager to get out in the sun and onto that glorious, clean beach outside the hotel.

Rick was sitting next to me, legs outstretched, working diligently on his laptop. And so, while I waited for him to finish so we could go enjoy the sand and surf, I decided to crack open my own laptop and do, I dunno, something (you know how it is, there's always "something"). And as often happens when you open a gadget to do "something," I unconsciously clicked on Facebook for just a moment.

Immediately, I saw a slew of posts of my friends and family living their best lives, and one picture in particular caught my eye. And in that split second, my lightness and eagerness dipped, my stomach sank just a little, and I distinctly remember the following conversation in my own head. A tiny mewing voice said:

Oh wow, I wish I was there.

Followed immediately by a louder, more powerful voice in my head saying,

ANJALI. WHAT THE ACTUAL FUCK.

Here I was in paradise, one of my favorite places in the world, with the love of my life at a luxury hotel miraculously paid for thanks to him being, ya know, an international rock star and all, on a perfect sunny day, and I wanted to be *somewhere else*? Nope. I didn't. But fabulous fucking FOMO—that awful, insidious asshole—had reared its ugly head and shown up. On my vacation.

FOMO. Fear Of Missing Out.

Just like that unwanted guest we didn't invite to the party but who somehow always finds out where it's at, FOMO seems to show up at the most unwanted and unnecessary times. I mean, the fact is, there's *never* really a time when FOMO is wanted or necessary because its only function is to take us *out* of the present and *out* of gratitude. Two of the most important places to be *in* in our lives.

A friend of mine once said, "Yeah, right now I'm suffering from FOMO's asshole cousin, IKIMO: I *know* I'm missing out," and thanks to social media, that is probably a little more accurate to what I and so many of us feel in these moments—the lamenting of not being somewhere else instead of being where we are. FOMO and IKIMO are like a duo of bank robbers stealing our fun. Taken to a further degree, FOMO and IKIMO both come down to one thing: wishing away *life*. And I think it's pretty clear that that is, well, not something we want to do.

Walking to work one day when I had just started the *I Am Fun Size* series, I was talking to my dear friend, Caroline Kinsolving (contributor to two of my favorite episodes, but more than that, a wise and loving contributor to my life). I was lamenting that I couldn't do a particular acting job because I was going to be working on the beautiful play I was in the process of performing at the time, and she just said these six words: "Trust the timing of your life." It was the perfect little snap-out-of-it moment that reminded me of two things: I am so lucky to be alive where and when I am, and I must relish the place I currently am.

We are faced with way more information these days about the comings and goings of others. The more you are on social media, the more of other people's lives you are seeing. But every time you see those posts or tweets or videos and lament not being able to do something or getting to go somewhere, you are taking the *fun* out of your own life. When you are busy looking to those sources to see what you "should" be doing, you are busy NOT living the big, beautiful life right in front of you.

Even without social media, it's hard enough to say no to things in order to say yes to something else. We are taught in so many ways in today's society that in order to be happy, we must find a way to have and do as much as possible. In recent years, I've learned nothing could be further from the truth. As hard as it may be to accept, saying yes to something is saying no to something else (at least until we can clone ourselves and somehow experience multiple lifetimes all at once, which, ya know, I'm all about if someone wants to get on that). But the goal isn't to get over what we're saying no to, it's to make sure to say *yes* to what we truly want and to be where we are.

I'll say that again. Be. Where. You. Are.

When my husband and I were first dating, there was a time when I had gone out to visit him on the road, and due to a particular set of circumstances he informed me I would have to split off from him on his tour for a few days. At the time, I was dismayed that I would have to peel myself away from his loving arms, even for just a few days. *(I mean, how on Earth can he take it*, I whined on the inside.) I decided I better do something spectacular so I wasn't pining away for an entire 96 hours.

Having been an avid indoor rock climber for many years when I lived in Chicago, I decided to have an adventure. I would take myself to Marseilles and do some rock climbing with a guide for three days in Les Calanques—the stunning cliffs off the coast of Cassis and Marseilles.

At the train station, I didn't want to leave him. I almost had to pry myself off him to get on the train. And every moment I had I wanted to share with him somehow through a message or a text or a call or *something*. But in my wisdom and awareness that no one wants to date Clingy McGee, I focused on the adventure at hand. And thank God I did because that trip was hands down the best gift I've ever given myself.

BE. WHERE. YOU. ARE.

I remember thinking at a random moment on the *very first day* out on the rock face, *Wow, this is the first time in months that when Rick and I have been apart, I'm truly not just wanting to be where he is. I'm perfectly happy where I am, and I have been this whole day.* Where I happened to be was hundreds of feet over the ocean climbing up a rock face and making sure I didn't plummet down to my death on the rocks below, but I was in *sheer bliss.*

The point is this: Being present in today's world is not easy. It only comes with protecting your focus and your energy and most of all, practicing wild and almost fanatical gratitude for where you are. No, it doesn't require a solo trip to the cliffs of Marseilles to be fanatically grateful. I've been fanatically grateful for where I am when I am alone in my pajamas in bed, when I am at work, when I am picking out the most fragrant spices for a meal I'm preparing, when I'm smelling Charley's paws as he snuggles in beside me in the middle of the night. (That delicious corn-chip-doggie-toe-beans smell is probably one of my favorite things in the world.)

No matter where we are, we can absolutely practice gratitude—for that moment, all the moments that came before to get us there, and all the moments it is leading us to. FOMO too easily steals the joy, the *fun* from our lives, steals away precious moments, steals away chances to learn, to see, to feel, to do. Nothing about wishing we were on that imaginary life path we see on social media is going to help us enjoy the here and now.

So, trust the timing of your life. Trust there is beauty and wonder in the here and now. Send FOMO (and IKIMO) packing and on their not-so-merry way. And then watch how much more Fun Size your life will become.

PART 2: THE MESSY MIDDLE

CAROLINA RAVASSA

ACTRESS/VOICE ACTRESS (OVERWATCH, VALORANT), COLOMBIANA, YOGINI, SALSA DANCING SENSATION, AND ONE OF THE BEST FRIENDS A PERSON COULD ASK FOR
WWW.IAMFUNSIZE.COM/CAROLINARAVASSA

"The Universe is going to give you what you need at the right time. And we have to trust that. I think about it for acting a lot. Perhaps I wasn't ready for a certain role and that's why I didn't book it; maybe I needed to learn a few things before. I think the right things come to the right people, too. If a friend books something, then that was meant for her and something else is meant for me. We have to believe in that. We just have to trust that everything comes at its right time."

REGAINING FAITH IN YOURSELF AFTER TOUGH TIMES

Ah, failure. Honestly, of all the words in the English language that have caused more unnecessary fear and guilt and self-flagellation, this has got to be in the top three. The fear of failure can tap into our most primal fear of death, and our beautiful subconscious brain thinks failure is actually a bloodthirsty tiger that's going to eat us alive. (More on this in Part 3.) Yet some of the greatest growth and course correction comes *precisely* at that moment when we "fail" and have to figure out what to do next.

But how do you regain faith in yourself to make the right decision after you've made one that caused so much grief/pain/anxiety/general awfulness? Well, let me start with a little kinesiology.

When I was about to graduate college, being the wildly unathletic but still health-conscious person that I was, I decided that I wanted to get certified as a personal trainer. Not only would this give me a way to earn money, set my own schedule, and be appreciated for the knowledge and services I provided, it was also something that intrigued me deeply from a personal standpoint because a) I wanted to share with others equally as unathletic as I was how to be healthy and fit without having to be great at sports, and b) I may not have followed in my parents' footsteps to be a doctor, but I still had a passion for learning about the human body—how it worked, why it worked the way it did, and how we could do whatever it took to keep it healthy. During my years of dance in college, I had sprained my ankle more times than I could count, and I wanted to learn more about the ways I could rehabilitate my body and recover faster so I was injuring myself less and enjoying being active more.

Throughout my studies, I learned about a vital concept in rehab and post-rehab exercise programs: the concept of proprioception, also known as kinesthesia. Proprioception is your awareness of where you are in space without necessarily having to look at yourself to see where you are. It's what enables dancers to maintain a perfect shape in space without having to see where they are, enables a mom to reach behind her to tousle her child's hair while talking on the phone, enables us to walk down a flight of stairs to reunite with our family without looking at our feet.

When we injure ourselves—let's use the example of the sprained ankle—not only are our tendons and ligaments torn and in need of healing, but the neural pathways between our skeletal system and proprioceptive awareness need to be retrained as well. So, while we're icing and resting and strengthening and stretching, we also do things like balancing on one foot and then doing it with our eyes closed to rediscover how to maintain that balance without seeing the world around us for reference.

And you better believe that part of the process is *hard*. I was always amazed how I could balance perfectly with my eyes open after an injury, but the second my eyes closed, I was as wobbly as a Weeble. It took time, patience, and a lot of deep breathing through the frustration to build that back up after every time I hurt myself. But each time, the neural pathways fired right back up with more and more use.

So, what does this have to do with royally screwing something up and not trusting yourself to get it right again? Everything. When we screw up in life, we have to build back our *emotional* proprioception. When we fail at something, or even when we don't fail but somehow something in the world happens to rock our faith, we lose our sense of where we are in the world, in space. We need to rebuild those neural pathways that believe we've got this. And we need to be gentle with ourselves while we rebuild. Just like we wouldn't go run a marathon on that ankle the next day, we take our time and support ourselves through the journey. We ice and rest the emotional pain of pushing through the fear of failing or being hurt again.

WHEN WE SCREW UP IN LIFE, WE HAVE TO BUILD BACK OUR EMOTIONAL PROPRIOCEPTION.

So, how do we rebuild emotional proprioception? Well, one of the things we do in physical therapy to retrain an injured ankle is to stand on that one leg on a wobble board or even just a soft surface like a carpet. The key is to put yourself on an uneven surface and train your muscles and the neural pathways in your body to adjust to keep you balanced. When you first try it post injury, your leg wobbles like a six-month-old child trying to walk for the first time. And then, here's the doozy, as it gets easier, you try closing your eyes. Suddenly, it's just you and your ankle and the input it gets from *actually* physically being where it is.

When we lose the sense of self we might have had before an emotional shock (e.g., loss of a loved one, breakup, health trauma), it's important to metaphorically close our eyes and clock where we are and who we are *inside ourselves*.

This is what I had to do at the end of that long, deeply emotional breakup with "Danny" I mentioned earlier in the book. While it was absolutely right to end it for my own self-preservation, I genuinely felt like I didn't know who I was without the relationship. It was as if the ground had disappeared from under me. I wasn't mourning the loss of the person in my life as much as the loss of my understanding of what my life was and who I was when I was connected to this person. I found I was not trusting myself, not liking myself, not believing in myself.

I knew I was a big, powerful personality at heart, but I felt so small on the inside. I didn't trust myself or my "picker" when it came to relationships, and I didn't entirely trust I would find happiness again at all. Suffice it to say in terms of our analogy here, it was a third-degree ankle sprain with a very, very dicey prognosis and a long bout of physical therapy and rehab ahead.

To start recovering, it took me really "closing my eyes" to whatever I had perceived as defining my life before and looking at what my life was now and rediscovering myself. What things were a constant before and after him, and what no longer served me? What were the things I actually liked, not the things I had learned to like because he did? What did I truly care about? What did I want to do when I didn't have to think of someone else? What gave *me* joy? What was *fun* for me?

I kept thinking of the end of the movie, *Runaway Bride*, with Julia Roberts (spoiler alert in case you haven't seen it and are planning a night in with Netflix for a Gere-Roberts marathon). At one point in the movie, Richard Gere's character points out to Julia Roberts's character that she changes the kind of eggs she orders depending on the man she is with. And when she leaves him at one point in the movie, after a rather blunt talking-to from Mr. Gere, she realizes she has no idea what kind of eggs she actually likes.

So, she sits down to a giant table of different preparations of eggs, and when she finally returns to our leading man (in true Hollywood fashion), she declares her final choice, which is incidentally the same as mine: Eggs Benedict (only I like mine with salmon and spinach instead of Canadian bacon if anyone's planning to surprise me with brunch soon).

Just like Julia's egg experiment, my wobble board training included a lot of gentle exploration of what I liked, believed, trusted, and enjoyed. And much like in physical therapy, I had to be *very* gentle and patient with myself as I learned where I was in emotional space. If I could only hold myself together for a few minutes before bursting into tears, it was like holding that wobble board balance for a short time. I was in training and had to give myself the leeway to make progress from scratch.

I would tell myself, *It's fine if you cry all day, you just have to do it while you're doing the dishes or working on things or somehow moving, not curled up in a ball in bed.* It was basic, tiny steps into finding who I was on my own. I trained on that metaphorical wobble board a little more each day until, one day in May, one of my best friends told me, "I don't know what's going on, but there is something about your energy right now that is more confident and attractive than I've ever seen you, and I'm excited for you."

And guess what? Just a few days later, I met a little dog named Charley at a farmer's market, fell in love with his adorable little self, and adopted him (my very first dog). Two days later, I auditioned for a musical written by and starring a fellow named Ty Taylor where I met a certain bass player named Rick Barrio Dill who was in the band. And since I finally knew what kind of eggs I loved, so to speak, since I'd learned where I was in emotional space after practicing on that wobble board for months, I actually had an open enough heart to be able to follow the path that was right for me, and run that marathon to the life I have today.

It may make me a bit of a science geek, but I've found it very useful to think of proprioception when learning to trust myself or the world after being deeply hurt, whether by others or myself. Give yourself the gift of understanding as you are finding where you are in space again, and be patient as you find your way to balance, and then walking, and then running, and then leaping, all over again.

GIVE THE PAIN A PURPOSE

The pain was unbearable—mostly because it wasn't mine to bear, and I didn't know how to stop it. It was years ago and I was watching one of the finest people I have ever met on this planet imploding emotionally, physically, and mentally because of the pain they felt over the end of a very long and loving relationship. They had admittedly caused a tremendous amount of pain to both themselves and their now ex-partner, mostly because of their indecision borne of the desire to cause *less* pain and somehow make the relationship work. As one friend put it to them, by not ending the relationship clearly and cleanly, "You say you would take a bullet for this person, but instead, you're spraying bullets everywhere."

This person was so full of self-loathing for the decision they had finally made and how they had done it, and I was watching them fall apart in so many ways. They were feeling so unworthy of happiness because of the pain they had caused, but they had made this decision in the name of finding *greater* happiness in their own life. They were paralyzed by the stalemate, falling deeper and deeper into self-destructive behaviors to cope with it. And it was heartbreaking to watch it.

The only thing I could offer in that moment were the words I'm going to share here—probably said a lot less eloquently at the time, and definitely through tears, but with no less certainty and conviction.

It's an unfortunate fact of life, but at some point (probably many points), we are going to have to experience pain—physical, emotional, mental, you name it. And quite likely, we are going to cause some pain, too. None of us is infallible. Sometimes in moments of reactivity or not-so-evolved behavior, we actually choose to act in ways that we know might hurt people, and hardest of all (for me at least), sometimes the things we know we need to do for ourselves cause suffering to someone else who is affected by that choice. Pain is a fact of life, and it's something we can't always avoid, although many try to in unhealthy ways.

So, what can we do to make pain bearable without running from it? And what can we do when we've caused pain to others, either purposely or by mistake?

We can give the pain a purpose.

Now, a personal note here: While I know many people take solace in saying, "Everything happens for a reason," or "God doesn't give us more than we can handle," I am personally way too much of a control freak to leave my fate completely up to someone or something else. I do believe in a compassionate and beautiful Universal Energy that we all come from and return to, but I don't believe that I am a marionette in its hands, and that my road has been preordained.

This means if there is a reason that I am going through

something, it's up to *me* to decide what it is. And more often than not, it's not always clear in the moment. But looking back, I can often connect the dots from that painful moment to an extraordinary moment and see how one wouldn't have happened without the other. It's bridging the gap between that painful moment I'm *in* and the future moment I *will be in* that makes that pain bearable.

But what about in the moment when the pain is so bad that I can't see what good could possibly come from it?

BUT LOOKING BACK, I CAN OFTEN CONNECT THE DOTS FROM THAT PAINFUL MOMENT TO AN EXTRAORDINARY MOMENT AND SEE HOW ONE WOULDN'T HAVE HAPPENED WITHOUT THE OTHER.

There is always at least *one* good thing that can come from going through any experience, positive or negative, wildly blissful or impossibly tragic. It is that going through something builds your compassion for and understanding of others who have gone through or are going through the same thing. We don't need to experience pain to have compassion or understanding, but there is a level of both that come from knowing what it feels like. And if you tell yourself that in the moment, it moves the needle just a little bit from unbearable to tolerable. It can provide even the smallest bit of solace.

Give the pain a purpose, even if it is just compassion for now. Maybe the pain was necessary for you to see something that was lacking in your life or that you had your priorities mixed up. Maybe the pain was just enough of a wake-up call for you to look at your life and see that you were off-track somehow from your own desires, morals, or dreams. Maybe the pain was there to slow you down. Whatever it is, you get to choose how you see it and how you use it.

We aren't the sum of what has happened to us in our lives, where we were born, or who we were born to. We are the sum of what we have taken from what we've experienced and how we *choose* to move through the world because of it (or in spite of it). Some of the world's most powerful healers, leaders, and innovators have made their contributions because they went through some kind of pain that they wanted to make better for others and/or make sense of for themselves.

The archetype of the wounded healer is all over our mythology and our reality. Caroline Myss speaks of this archetype in her spellbinding book, *Sacred Contracts: Awakening Your Divine Potential:*[7] "The Wounded Healer archetype emerges in your psyche with the demand that you push yourself to a level of inner effort that becomes more of a process of transformation than an attempt to heal an illness. If you have successfully completed the initiation, you inevitably experience exceptional healing, and a path of service seems to be divinely provided shortly after the initiation is complete."

From Mahatma Gandhi to Maya Angelou to Oprah Winfrey and more, there are numerous stories of people who took the circumstances of their own struggle and turned them into fuel to make other people's journeys easier. And through that gift to the world, they continued to heal their own pain.

Ask yourself, "What do I know now, having experienced this pain, that I didn't know before? Can I help someone else with this knowledge? Can I release this pain, even just a little bit, knowing that with time, I will make sense of it in my story as I continue to write it with love and compassion for myself?" The answers to these questions can help you give a purpose to your pain that's meaningful and valuable for you, if you focus on the direction they are guiding you toward, instead of looking back at the cause of your pain, even if it was your own doing.

But what do we do if we have *caused* pain that we need or want to make better? And how on Earth can we give purpose to *that*?

I'm sure you've heard the trope, "Living well is the best revenge." I believe the flipside of that truth is, "Doing better is the best apology." While one is a way forward after someone has hurt you, the other is a way forward after you have caused another pain.

Yes, it is an unfortunate truth that sometimes, somewhere along the line, following our own dreams and desires comes in direct conflict with the needs or wants of someone else. It could be leaving a relationship that someone else doesn't want to end, choosing a career path that your family disapproves of but you know is the one for you, or just simply wanting something different than a loved one wants. One way or another, as we pursue a Fun Size life, there will be a moment (or several) where our choices—right though they may be—cause someone else pain. What on Earth can we do when we are so torn between choosing what is right for us and what might be right for someone else?

I'll tell you first what *doesn't* help: being so mired down in guilt and self-flagellation that we have one leg in what was, one leg in what might be, and no progress toward the biggest Fun Size life we are aiming to lead. Because the truth is, being fuller, bigger, happier, better is just about the best thing you can do for the world. Why? Because the better we feel about ourselves, the more empowered we are to help others around us.

Now let's look at what *does* help to heal the pain we might have caused: We can *do better*. We can be better than we were in the situation that was keeping us small, keeping us broken, keeping us "fine" but not powerfully happy. We can do more good in the world by leading by example. We can accept responsibility for the pain we have caused, and yes, make amends where we can, but after that first period of guilt, we *must* forgive ourselves and just do better next time.

If you indeed broke someone's heart to find a better relationship, what good is it for you to be so racked with guilt that you don't pursue with all your heart the very thing you left to find? If you have indeed disappointed your family by choosing a career they didn't want you to pursue, what good is it for you to feel so guilty that you can't succeed at the path you did choose because you're constantly thinking about making them sad?

While I know many of us have experienced for ourselves or been on the receiving end of that feeling of wanting someone who hurt us to hurt as much as we do in return, I genuinely believe that's just a mistaken belief that someone else's pain will alleviate ours. Our pain is our responsibility as much as our own happiness is. The only way to single-handedly pursue a bigger life and simultaneously help those around us—even those who may wish we are hurting as much as they are—is to be self-forgiveness ninjas. We can live by example, not by regret.

OUR PAIN IS OUR RESPONSIBILITY AS MUCH AS OUR OWN HAPPINESS IS.

This doesn't mean we condone shitty behavior, especially our own; nowhere in the definition of forgiveness is there a section that says, "Forgiveness means letting the forgiven off the hook." But it does mean we let go of the shackles that keep us tied to that pain, to that shitty behavior, to that very difficult but necessary thing we don't want to have to do again. As my trainer, Eddie, says, "Don't say sorry, just fix it." It's not a smackdown, it's a very short and sweet way to say if you know you got something wrong, don't waste energy feeling like crap about it any longer than you truly have to. Instead, change it and do better.

Most of all, forgiving ourselves and doing better gives the world around us permission to be imperfect. If I were judged today on some of the mistakes I've made in the past (or forget the mistakes, the genuinely *wrong* things I did knowing full well they were wrong at the time but thinking they would bring me happiness or love or any number of things in the moment), I would dissolve into a useless puddle. It's precisely *because* I have failed in so many ways (many of which are in this book) that I've been free to learn and grow and most of all, *share my experiences* so others can learn from them, too. But without allowing forgiveness into the picture, that sharing, that community, that uplifting others in need *cannot happen*.

So again, take that pain of yours—and yes, the pain of having to sometimes leave others behind—and honor it and make it worthwhile by living the biggest, fullest, most generous life you can, and helping others to do the same.

WHATEVER THE WEATHER

I remember the first time I read about sunburn as a child. I must have been about eight years old, flipping through an American Red Cross handbook. (Look, I was a precocious kid and way ahead of the Girl Scouts with their whole "be prepared" thing. My parents put me in charge of the fire safety plan for the family, and once I was done with it, it was as complex and perfect as the heist in *Ocean's Eleven*).

Suddenly, a very specific bit of information that was bolded and italicized caught my eye: "You can even get a sunburn on a cloudy day." I remember thinking how crazy it was that the sun was so powerful that even when we couldn't see it or feel its warmth directly, it was shining so brightly behind those clouds that it had the same effect then as it had when I was out by the pool with my friends, slathered in chalky, white sunscreen on my smooth, dark skin. From that moment on and to this day, I've got my sunscreen on 365 days a year (although there were probably an awful lot of subzero temperature days while I lived in Chicago and you couldn't see an inch of my skin underneath all the layers of parka, polar fleece, sweater, long underwear, and tank top that I might have forgone that little precaution).

But one of the other wondrous things about that statement that has stuck with me and I often remind myself of is that no matter what it looks like outside—whether there is a thunderstorm or blizzard or rain or wind—that beautiful sun is still up there providing light and warmth to us here on Planet Earth, allowing plants to grow, powering our world, keepin' on keepin' on. Which is a wonderful reminder for how the Universe, no matter what is going on in your world, is still up there and out there and around us listening. Creating things you can't see yet but that are on their way, putting together the pieces to create things you've asked for and have been working toward. Just because you're having a rough time doesn't mean the sun stops shining behind the clouds, and it definitely doesn't mean the Universe isn't out there conspiring for your greatest good.

"Oof, Anj, skip the woo-woo. I'm feeling crappy, and if we're talking about my life as if it were a weather forecast, today it's cloudy with a 100% chance of thunderstorms leaking out my eyeballs."

Okay, friend. I hear that. So, if you wanna skip the woo-woo for a minute, let's flip the script and look at it like a big stage play or a musical with sets and lights and automation and all sorts of amazing things that are still happening behind the scenes to make the play of your life a masterpiece. And let's imagine that what's creating said oeuvre for your enjoyment are all the people in your world, the plans you've set in motion, and the hard work you've done up to this point to build a life you love.

I can tell you from firsthand experience that in order for that onstage magic to happen, there is a whole other production—often ten times more complicated than what you are seeing—going on behind the scenes. That quick change that makes it possible for the leading lady to transform from a beggar woman into a duchess in under 60 seconds? It's a crazy whirlwind of three dressers and the actress doing some of the most insanely complicated dressing choreography you can imagine. And a lot of the time, it's *not* graceful.

Said actress might have to drop trou with the help of two people ripping her clothes off her, run down a flight of stairs to the backstage crossover, run across the length of the stage, run back up a flight of stairs to meet the other three dressers who are holding a complicated corseted gown and wig and shoes, get it on her body as fast as physically possible, take a breath as the last hook is secured on the bodice, grab her prop fan, and glide out on the stage as if it ain't no thang, and then the audience goes wild. (It's moments like these that made it possible for me to avoid going to the gym for about 10 years; performing eight shows a week was my workout every night.)

All of that is happening while pulleys are being pulled and gears are being turned to seamlessly change the set for the next scene, but when you are out in the audience watching, the result can seem miraculous. "How did they do that? It was so smooth. I had no idea that was coming!" and on the play goes.

If as an audience member you were despairing, upset, worried that the stage might catch on fire, having a terrible time, guess what would still happen? The same smooth transition. Because the play goes on.

So, in both of these instances, just a little reminder: Whatever the weather, until some insane force of science changes the course of our solar system forever, the sun is still up there shining, and no matter what you might see happening in your own life, no matter if there are bad moods and obstacles and daunting events, highs and lows and diagonals, there are still forces that you can't see working on those very goals and dreams you have set forth.

All you have to do is keep going, taking one step after the other, moving through that tough time and trusting that each of your inspired actions is contributing to what you want to create. Bad day, good day, sunshine, rain, you name it. Whatever the weather, the sun is still out there shining its good ol' rays down and powering the world.

(And yeah, don't forget sunscreen.)

PART 2: THE MESSY MIDDLE

JOSH PETERSDORF
VOICE ACTOR (OVERWATCH, AGGRETSUKO), LOVING HUSBAND AND FATHER, AND INSPIRATIONAL AND HIGH-SPIRITED FELLA
WWW.IAMFUNSIZE.COM/JOSHPETERSDORF

"I would tell my younger self believe in who you are. Don't get discouraged and know that there's a light at the end of that tunnel. A lot of us go through some dark paths, but trust me, there's rays of hope that fall around. And in the words of Optimus Prime: 'Fate rarely calls upon us at a moment of our choosing.' Everybody, believe you can do it and believe you're worth it because you are the best you that you can be.

Part 3

The Home Stretch

"WHEN IT'S YOUR DESTINY, IT'S NOT ABOUT LUCK.
IT'S ABOUT ENDURANCE."

— TY TAYLOR

How to Get Over Underestimating Yourself (with Love to Sara Bareilles)

I received this honest, relatable gem of a question about two years into doing *I Am Fun Size* and could not wait to answer it, although it would also involve sharing one of my favorite personal stories publicly for the first time. That said, this felt like the perfect time to use my personal experience to help someone else. This is what the email said:

> "Here we go. I'm 21 now, and I'm starting this year to study at college and work with what I love. When it comes to doing some academic work that's less hard, but for real work, like real people that hire me, I underestimate myself too much. I have in my head that I learned what I knew in college with the best teachers, I did exercises, had exams, my grades were great, but when it comes to applying all of that for real, I suddenly get insecure. I get myself together and do it anyway and the results are often great, but still, I have this feeling every time in every work I do, I have this big feeling of failure. If I say I know I can do this and in the end I can't, I let people down and they'll never trust me again for doing something like that in the future. So I end up not taking risks, and that sucks because later when it's all done by someone else, I realize that I could really do it but I

didn't. So I'm sending you this email to ask what I'm supposed to think and how I'm supposed to act when I get this feeling again."

This doubt, this fear creeping into this brilliant young mind is something we *all* face, no matter how far down the career/life path we are. Seriously, 20 years into my career with numerous plays, TV shows, movies, etc. under my belt, I *still* feel like an imposter sometimes when I get ready for an audition. I still battle that paralyzing fear when I try something new. Why? Well, there's actually a scientific explanation, believe it or not.

There's this amazing part of our beautiful, brilliant brain called the amygdala. Its main job is to perceive threat and make sure we survive it. (You may have heard of the flight/fight/freeze response. That's the amygdala's main job.) There's just one problem. The amygdala was built to perceive and react to threats like being eaten by a tiger or falling off a cliff. And it can sometimes perceive *any* threat (say, the threat of failing miserably in a job interview) as just as serious as startling an angry, starving tiger. In fact, the amygdala overreacts to these modern-day threats so often that author and psychologist Daniel Goleman,[8] coined the term "amygdala hijack" for this very occurrence.

It stands to reason, then, that this part of the brain can be triggered when we are afraid of being abandoned or disappointing people, or of someone not loving or trusting us anymore. This is because one of our greatest needs as humans is the need for connection. When you feel that seemingly irrational fear, understand that this is your brain doing *exactly* what it's supposed to do. It's pushing you not to change, not to branch out into new adventures because it is trying to keep you alive. And so far, it's doing a great job because here you are, reading this book—good job, brain! The trick is training our mind, subconscious and conscious, to know what is a real threat and what is just a perceived threat.

One of my tried-and-true ways of outsmarting my amygdala is to say yes to doing scary things. I've made a pact with myself to do something uncomfortable every day, something that scares me once a month, and something that downright terrifies me once a year. So, let me tell you about the thing that terrified me in 2016.

I had been struggling with some very confusing issues with my voice for a few years, which was a long time to be feeling this, physically and emotionally, especially given the career I've chosen. Somehow, my incredibly dependable vocal cords were giving out on me after just the littlest of vocal exertion. Where I used to be able to handle speaking over a loud crowd for hours or singing for two hours straight during a performance, now there seemed to be a 50/50 chance on any given night that I would be unable to talk by the end of the night. I went to three different voice specialists who gave me three different diagnoses, but no matter what I tried, it was still happening.

As a singer for most of my life—musicals, opera, rock, pop, you name it—as well as a theatre actress used to doing eight shows a week with no trouble, this was a truly awful feeling. It struck me at my core and rocked my very identity. Even though I did performances here and there, I was living in a place of worry and fear that somehow my voice would give out, and sure enough, I was singing less and less, even speaking less and less in my day-to-day life. I was feeling smaller and smaller. This very basic form of expression became an emotional battle for me every time I performed, every time I even *spoke*. The fear was making me the opposite of Fun Size for sure. I was feeling very, very small. Almost like I was disappearing.

Then one day, my agents called me with an audition for the musical, *Waitress* on Broadway. In the room would be the casting director, the director, and the writer/creator of the show, Sara Bareilles. If you don't know anything about Sara Bareilles, suffice it to say she has not only one of the most beautiful voices there is, but her artistry, her writing, and how much of herself she puts into everything she creates is wildly inspiring.

ONE OF MY TRIED-AND-TRUE WAYS OF OUTSMARTING MY AMYGDALA IS TO SAY YES TO DOING SCARY THINGS.

Many people just knew her then because of the hits she'd had on the radio (now she's got her hands in pretty much every artistic medium there is and is excelling at all of them), but I also loved her because of the energy I could feel when I heard her speak. This was a genuinely artistic being, someone who put herself out there into the world to create from her heart and soul, and there was no chance in hell I was going to miss the opportunity to meet her.

However, you wouldn't believe the train of fearful thoughts that followed me getting the audition (hi, remember me talking about self-in-spiral-ing?): *I can't, my voice is broken. I can't sing anymore. I haven't sung. I'll have to fly out to New York, and I'll embarrass myself and I probably won't even book the job anyway.*

But instead of spiraling down that whirlpool of hell, I reminded myself of my *why*:

> *Anj. There's no way you're missing the chance to meet Sara. So here we go. Worst-case scenario is you embarrass yourself and they never call you back in for an audition for this casting office ever again. Okay, you're not dead. That is not a great outcome, but you'll live. Best case scenario, you book the job; unlikely but that's a thing. Other best case scenario? You prove to yourself that you can do it. You prove to your new agents that you can do it. And they continue to send you these great auditions for leading roles on Broadway. No matter what, you get a chance to meet this incredible artist and tell her how special she is and hopefully get to convey to her how much what she does means to you.*

Part 3: The Home Stretch

To say the process of working on the audition was an emotional one is a wild understatement. Rick is a world-class musician for goodness' sake, and we are surrounded by world-class singers every day. With all that was going on with my voice, I was afraid and embarrassed to sing even around him. Never mind that we had met years earlier when I was singing in the show I mentioned earlier, and that he often reflects on it, saying that performance is when he began falling for me because I brought tears to his eyes every night.

While you would think that would alleviate my concern of what he thought of me, it instead made the fear worse since I was so convinced that, *That was then, this is now; my voice is broken. If he heard me sing now, he wouldn't feel that way.* Oof. Fear is a bitch, and that amygdala of mine was *convinced* there was a tiger in the room, waiting to pounce.

Shaking in our 523-square-foot apartment, I told Rick, "I have to do this audition, and I'm fucking terrified. I need you to go in the other room while I sing and I need you to *not* listen. I'm going to put on my headphones and sing, and just please, say nothing to me about it. Let me sing. Don't tell me it's good. Don't tell me it's bad. Just don't even listen."

The first time I opened my mouth to sing the audition song, the fear was monumental. But so was the release. Shaking and crying, I allowed all of this emotion to pour out while I did what I knew I had to do—not for the audition, not for

Sara Bareilles, but for *me*. I needed to sing because it is part of who I am, part of my soul being freed to express itself, and I couldn't let this fear stop that anymore. It was a level of fear I hadn't had as a performer in my entire life, and haven't had since. And it wasn't even in front of an audience; it was in front of *myself*.

I pushed through that evening, worked with a vocal coach on the song, and prepared as best as I knew how for the audition. Then, I hopped on a plane to New York to see the show before I auditioned. It was glorious. Jessie Mueller as the lead was utterly spectacular, as was the whole cast, and I was unexpectedly relieved to see that the woman playing the role I was going in for was so different from me. There was no way I would be like her. I knew for sure the only way I could do this audition was my way—my interpretation, my sound. My personal motto of "success through lowered expectations" served me well because having no expectation that I would book the job, I didn't care if I did. I just needed to prove this to myself, and of course, meet Sara.

Knowing that I would be nervous (and admittedly not want to make it weird when I went in), I wrote Sara a handwritten card telling her how much I admire her as an artist and thanking her for all the beauty she puts into the world through her art and her openness. And I told myself, *Remember, all you have to do is survive.*

I wish I could say I remember the audition itself more. All

PART 3: THE HOME STRETCH

I remember is that Sara was even more lovely in person than I would have imagined. The whole room was very warm and kind. I wish I could say I went in and nailed it, knocked it out of the park, but honestly, the way I remember it, I sang fine. I was nervous, so probably not my finest work ever, but certainly my best in the moment. But most important I did it. I survived it. My voice not only didn't break, it showed up and let me express what I was experiencing in the world—excitement and fear and nervous anticipation of wanting something so badly you're afraid to have it—which was actually very apropos to the song I was singing (called "When He Sees Me"). I said my thanks and left the room, and on the way out, I handed the card to the casting associate, asked him to deliver it to Sara for me, and left the building.

Amazingly, I went home and didn't really think about it. I

simply gave myself a pat on the back and said, *Okay, you did it and you gave her the card, so you accomplished what you set out to do, and no one laughed at you or left you out of the room. And if they thought you sucked, they didn't tell you, so, great. You have achieved what you came out here to achieve.*" Done and done.

No, I didn't book the job. But stick with me. There is a happy ending.

A few weeks later, I received this message from Sara through my agents:

"Hey Anjali...

Thank you so much for taking the time to so thoughtfully share your feelings about my music with me. It always means so much to me to hear if my work has touched someone, and it especially means a lot when it's someone as talented as you. I so enjoyed getting a chance to see you do what you do, you were so creative and you sing absolutely beautifully. I wish you all the very best in your endeavors. You are a bright light and it is a great honor to know that you enjoy what I do. Thank you sincerely.

xoxo sara"

I still have that email sitting on my computer desktop.

Yes, it's a very long story, so why am I telling it? Because if I had let my fear of being unqualified—an imposter laughed off the stage—stop me, I would not have received this incredible gift from the Universe and from this very gracious, incredible artist who treated me not as someone less than, as I had been feeling, but as a peer, a fellow artist. *She said I am an artist and I am talented and* Sara Bareilles *sees that in me.* That kind of validation in that moment mattered more to me than booking the role.

I started singing again that week and—surprise, surprise—I found that my voice issues became less and less of a problem. I had to manage some limitations (like, duh, don't go to a crazy loud, crowded place and expect to talk over everyone and not lose your voice), and work a little more slowly back into it, but soon I was back to singing with the joy I had before, with the same endurance and vigor, and it has continued to give me joy ever since. Miraculously (but not at all surprisingly knowing how much the mind and body are connected), my voice hasn't failed me again. It has been there through thick and thin, even when I've overworked it. That fear was living on my vocal cords, on my neck, on my everything. Letting it go gave me the freedom to rebuild and rediscover the voice I'm meant to have, not the one I thought I was supposed to have.

We all want to hear that we are okay and that we're safe and that we're good, but we're not always going to get that back from the Universe. We certainly aren't if we don't say yes, or if we scare ourselves into paralysis and let other people step forward who may not even be as talented or smart as we are. We'll lose out to them because they had the metaphorical balls to put themselves forward regardless.

Incidents like this one with Sara and others in my life have taught me that I may not know what's going to come, but I can believe it's going to be more powerful than whatever the (highly unlikely) worst-case scenario could be.

So to that gem of a question, my answer is, open yourself up to the possibility that you are not only good enough to do the thing, but good enough to do the thing incredibly well. Believe that you are doing yourself *and the world around you* a service by putting yourself out there. You are a unique person who has this unique thing to give and learn from. You will grow from mistakes and you will grow from failures. That's *life*. Please don't let your tiger-fearing, screaming amygdala keep you from saying yes to your big, beautiful, Fun Size life.

One last epilogue...

In 2019, I was thrilled to be cast in a role in for Sara's show on Apple TV+, *Little Voice*. And the very happiest part of shooting that show was being able to tell Sara this entire story, to thank her for bringing me back to singing. By taking the time to write that email, she had helped me get back on the path of happiness and fulfillment in my art. I am truly and endlessly grateful for that seemingly simple act. It's a reminder that *every* act of kindness any of us share can actually change a person's life.

Anjali Bhimani

JEN COHN
VOICE ACTRESS (OVERWATCH, STAR WARS: THE OLD REPUBLIC, THE LAST AIRBENDER), FASHION MAVEN, GAMING/FASHION/STYLE CONNECTOR, HOST OF THE ASK BIRDMOM STREAM, FLUENT FRENCH SPEAKER, AND SUPERMOM
WWW.IAMFUNSIZE.COM/JENCOHN

"Something my husband said to me when I was just starting to get a really good voiceover career going. And I was, like, really nervous about knocking on certain doors and about making things happen, just there were certain things that really frightened me. And he said to me, 'You know you can't treat your career like it's a delicate little egg. You can't be worried that every time if you do something wrong, that you're going to splat. You are not an egg, you a Tonka truck. You are a Tonka truck. And you need to be willing to smash into the wall. And you need to be willing to get dinged and get scratched and get dented. That is what makes a Tonka truck great. And a Tonka truck can withstand that. You are not an egg. You are a Tonka truck.' That changed everything."

TOUCHSTONES, SILLY SONGS, AND GOOD MORNINGS

If I had to choose, I'd definitely say I'm a morning person. Not like a spring-out-of-bed-skipping-downstairs-while-singing-to-the-birds-as-they-circle-my-head morning person, but I certainly enjoy the promise of a new day. It hasn't always been this way, and there have definitely been periods of time when mornings were rough—emotionally, physically, mentally—depending on where I was in my life. But one thing has remained constant: As long as I manage to include at least one thing in my morning that I love, no matter how small it is, I find myself somehow ready to overcome grogginess or stiffness or downright sadness at certain times because I've had that touchstone in my morning.

There have been thousands and thousands of pages written on the morning routines of great intellectuals, power players, athletes, business people, and superstars in our world, both past and present. And in trying to follow their lead, I have often found myself falling into a trap, a feeling that there is some perfect way to get my morning "right," and if somehow I do, I will unlock all of the secrets to massive success, happiness, and energy.

But for me, that's not how life works, and you know that's not how this book works. I've found there isn't any one perfect way for me to start the day; it changes and evolves just like I do. We are always evolving, always growing, always changing, and so the things that worked for us once might not work for us later. The thing that works for me on a Monday might not work for me on Wednesday.

But again, one thing does seem to always be valuable when I'm putting together my morning: If there's something that brings me joy, something *fun*, something that makes me smile, even for just 10 seconds, I'm on the right track to building the right morning. I might get derailed later, and often do, but even if I do, even if I have the most awful day, when I go to bed at night, I can stop and think about that one moment in the morning and lean into it as much as possible, remembering I've got another moment like that coming tomorrow.

So, in no particular order, here are some Fun Size morning touchstones I've used throughout my years that have brought me joy. I'm writing about them here because even talking about them brings me joy. Try them for yourself, or come up with your own. Remember, this is your life, and you get to play by your rules. I'm just tossing you different pieces of equipment to see what you like to play with the best (as well as some general things to avoid, in my experience).

FUN SIZE MORNING TOUCHSTONE #1: WHAT'S GOOD?

So much has been said about living in gratitude, practicing gratitude, doing a gratitude journal, but frankly it's become one of those words that I both love and hate. The way it gets weaponized as something we all *have* to do makes me cringe. In case you haven't noticed, I tend to get a bit indignant about people telling me what to do. If someone told me I can't eat broccoli for the rest of my life, you better believe I'll be eating broccoli by the ton by noon.

> "LOOK AROUND, LOOK AROUND AT HOW LUCKY WE ARE TO BE ALIVE RIGHT NOW."
> – HAMILTON, BY LIN-MANUEL MIRANDA

But when it comes to gratitude, gosh darn it, I have to admit—they are right. I've found that I like to trick myself into doing it using slightly different words and charging it with a little extra emotion. That's the point, right? To *feel* grateful? So in the morning, when I'm lying in bed, I might have a little dialogue with myself like this:

> *Oh my God, I can't believe how comfortable this bed is. How snuggly is this comforter? It's so warm and comfy and feels just right under my neck. Oh it's so, so good. And look at this adorable little nugget of a dog sleeping next to me! How lucky am I that this little bugger came into my life? Look at his little paws, they smell so good. And look at my Boo lying next to me. Look how cute his hair looks sticking out like that while he's sleeping peacefully. God, I'm a lucky woman. Ooh, look how nice the sun looks coming through the blinds like that even on an overcast day, that's good lighting...*

And then, we're off to the races...

For any of you who are struggling right now or have a knee-jerk response like, "That's easy for you, Anj, you have so much to be thankful for. I'm feeling so low right now I can barely think of anything." Guess what? It's not easy for me every day, and it definitely has not been easy for me at the lowest points in my life. But one way or another, I've done it. There have been days, many of them, when the most I could come up with that I genuinely felt gratitude for was my morning cup of coffee and my eyelashes. And no, there's nothing wrong with you (nor was there with me) when you have days like that.

> **THERE HAVE BEEN DAYS, MANY OF THEM, WHEN THE MOST I COULD COME UP WITH THAT I GENUINELY FELT GRATITUDE FOR WAS MY MORNING CUP OF COFFEE AND MY EYELASHES. AND NO, THERE'S NOTHING WRONG WITH YOU (NOR WAS THERE WITH ME) WHEN YOU HAVE DAYS LIKE THAT.**

But on those days and in those times, I have found that for me, it is *twice* as important to find something to be excited about and grateful for. That's when my system needs that jolt of positive energy the most. It's what breaks me out of the cycle of sad thoughts or spinning thoughts or just too many thoughts that could very well send me into a deeper depression if I don't get in there and do some cleaning up.

FUN SIZE MORNING TOUCHSTONE #2: CHARLEY'S MORNING SONG

I think parents (especially moms), caretakers, and animal owners can all relate to that awareness that no matter how important we make ourselves, sometimes there is another person or little creature who depends on us to take care of them first. We know there is no handling *anything* else until that little one's (or not-so-little one's) needs are met.

Thankfully, mine is the cutest little creature in the world, and so taking care of his needs actually fills me up first thing in the morning. When I got Charley, the early mornings when he would jump up the second I opened my eyes, as if to say, "You're awake? I'm awake! This is the best day ever!" were the most magical way to start the morning. Now that he's a little older, he likes to snuggle in a little bit, but every day still starts with that playful joy of him realizing it's time to go out. And since I was historically the morning person in the house, I like to be the one to get him up and out first thing. Even on my most tired days, it's a joy I relish so much.

For some people, taking care of someone else first feels like having to sacrifice, or having to put your needs aside. But for me, this short bit of the morning is 100% worth waking up a little earlier for, just to get in those extra snuggles, the belly rub, the prancing walk out the front door, and yes, to sing Charley's morning song: a little ditty I made up watching him prance happily down the street one morning at the crack of eggs.

This is one moment when I wish I could leap out of this book and make sound for you so you could hear it because it's a verified goddamn happy-maker. (And if I get to do the audiobook version at some point, you better believe I'm gonna sing it to you.) It's the closest I get to my Cinderella/Snow White moment every day. And I love it.

THE MORNING SONG

'Cuz it's the mor-ning

My fav'rite time of the day

And it's star-ting

In the very best way

First we're ea-ting

And then we're gon-na play

Today could be my fa-vo-rite day

(dun dun dun dun)

(Incidentally, we have a theme song for Charley as well, another ditty that popped out of my mouth one day and has stuck so hard-core that people sing it back to me on the reg. I think Charley and I might need a series soon, or at least an album. Hmmmm...)

FUN SIZE TOUCHSTONE #3: WHERE DO YOU WANT TO GO TODAY?

I've spoken many times in public about the joy that my coffee mug collection brings me. Somewhere around 2010,

PART 3: THE HOME STRETCH

I started collecting a very specific series of mugs from Starbucks—the Global Icon series, to be precise. Every time I went somewhere, I would swing by the ol' Starbucks and pick up a mug from that city or country or both to remind me of my time there. I may have gone to great lengths at times to get said mugs.

I remember on one road trip across the country to begin rehearsals for a play, I drove to three different Starbucks, each about 45 minutes from each other in the middle of Nebraska, trying to find an Omaha or a Lincoln mug, or even a Nebraska mug. (What I really should've done was look up on the internet if there was such an Omaha/Lincoln/Nebraska mug. There wasn't. Boo.)

I've only recently begun to have to seek them out online because the series was discontinued a few years ago, but every time I go somewhere new, I still find myself peering into a Starbucks just to check. I only pick mugs from places I've been, and with the exception of three of them, I have always done the purchasing myself.

Every morning, I make myself a hot beverage first thing, and I get to choose which memory to revel in. Do I go to Barcelona, where my husband and I have spent so many beautiful times together, and where I took that perfect picture of him and his mother in the Plaza Real? Do I go to Paris, which I first visited with my cousin Raj, who, having studied and lived there for three years, was not only fluent in French but seemed to know every nook and cranny of

243

Paris, and shared stories of not only its history, but of what movie was filmed on which corner and what scene to remember from it?

Do I go down to Orange County, where my dad bought me my hometown mug on one of our many car-wash-and-coffee dates that we used to take whenever I would visit? Do I go to Tampa, where Rick is from, and soak in the love I feel when I think of how this mug was the first gift my mother-in-love, Mamacita Carter, ever gave me? Or do I go back to Marseilles, where I took that incredible trip I mentioned earlier: rock climbing over the cliffs of the Mediterranean by day, eating bouillabaisse by night, and proving to myself how strong, adventurous, and happy I could be just being me?

Needless to say, this simple ritual of choosing a mug has become much more powerful than just bleary-eyed grabbing something out of the cabinet and sloshing coffee in it. What's more fun is that now when friends come over or when I make my husband a cup of coffee, I get to ask, "Where do you want to go today?" and share the magic with them. (Also, it's a great conversation starter at our dinner parties, and it keeps people from using someone else's mug).

Right now, as I'm writing this, I've pulled that Marseilles mug because when I asked myself where I wanted to go today, I wanted to go somewhere I can take you all with me. To a place where your day is full of untold possibility, or

PART 3: THE HOME STRETCH

where you can prove to yourself just how magical *you* are. Where, if you happen to be climbing a mountain and think you can't make it up, I know you'll prove yourself to be stronger than you know.

FUN SIZE TOUCHSTONE #4: MAKE THE DAY DELICIOUS

And now for what goes *in* the mug…

Things have changed over time, and while much has been said about the benefits and perils of drinking it, Mama has just got to have her coffee. I'm slightly embarrassed to admit that during a particularly low time in my life, when Cathleen was telling me something about coffee having a low vibration and affecting the vibration that we vibrate out or some such thing, I yelled back at her dramatically, "DON'T TAKE AWAY MY COFFEE. IT'S THE ONLY THING THAT MAKES ME HAPPY RIGHT NOW!"

Okay, so that was a bit extreme. Thankfully, she just said, "Uh oh. Okay, we'll put a pin in that," and let it slide.

But truly, it's about the ritual of having some kind of morning comfort. If I've left the snuggly warmth of my bed and decided to get up and face the day, I want a little bit of somethin', somethin' to make me feel cozy as I take on whatever challenges are ahead. So I make sure that my morning beverage is a straight-up treat. As is the ritual of making it.

Our coffee maker is probably my favorite appliance in the house. In case of emergency, I know I would need the refrigerator more, but I would be hard-pressed not to sacrifice it for this golden goose of a coffee maker. I'll make a little almond milk latte, caffeinated or decaf depending on the day. (And yes, during the fall, I will go full pumpkin spice latte with a little pumpkin stevia or actual pumpkin puree in it. I am *not* playin' with this morning coffee.)

Then, the *coup de grâce*, I'll write a message in cinnamon or pumpkin pie seasoning in the foam. It started with little love messages to Rick when I made his coffee in the morning (and when he was away from home, I would make the coffee, make the message, and send him a picture of it to make sure his day started with love), but then I started doing it for myself, too. Simple things I wanted to tell myself, and obviously they couldn't be too many words because there was only so much space.

Sometimes it was a drawing. Sometimes it was a sort of Rorschach test as to what I could see in the random swirls I had made that day, accented with lines made in that same ol' pumpkin pie spice. (I'm particularly proud of "Tall Smoking Man," "Woman with Fancy Hat," "Mafia Care Bear," and of course, "Charley with Bow Tie.") Other times it was a phrase I would carry through the day. *This is your day* or *You've got this* or simply *Breathe*. Nothing fancy, just something to keep me rolling strong (and to keep any of those less-than-helpful voices in my head at bay).

These days, I'm extra careful to drink a nice big cup of warm lemon water and a green drink before the coffee to make sure I get flushed out and get all my vitamins in, but once I get to that coffee—it's a beautiful way to fuel myself, not just with a drink I love, but with thoughts that make me happy, too.

FUN SIZE TOUCHSTONE #5: WHAT DO I GET TO DO TODAY? (AND SOME THOUGHTS ON WHAT NOT TO DO IN THE MORNING)

I am incredibly susceptible to the onslaught of busyness in the morning. Especially with cell phones and laptops and notifications, it's very easy to get overwhelmed as soon as we wake up, and I'm no stranger to this. Even if I don't turn on a single gadget, if I'm not careful, my mind will get ahead of me and start thinking of all the things I need to accomplish during the day. In short, my mind can turn the day into an assignment instead of a blessing, into one giant admin nightmare instead of an opportunity to live a big ol' Fun Size life.

I've been known, on my less well-managed mornings, to start the day grumbling about what's getting in the way of me enjoying the day, and suddenly, I find myself reading emails, getting caught up in admin tasks, calling customer service about something not that urgent, occasionally having to deal with a personal text sent the night before that is just *not* the way I want to start the day emotionally—all of this turning that beautiful feeling of gratitude and joy into a state of internal whining and railing at the technology gods for giving humanity the ability to do so much just with a cell phone.

That's why it's imperative for me *not* to check those gadgets first thing. Not only that, as I am preparing myself for whatever I have coming up, I approach it with the question, "What do I *get* to do today?" instead of, "What do I *have* to do today?" I usually don't even look at my day's calendar until I'm well into that cup of coffee, if not later. I do my best to take a peek at the calendar the night before so I'm already prepared for what's coming up tomorrow, and I can go to sleep knowing that I'll wake up ready.

I've been using this strategy a lot as I've been writing this book. I've woken up very early and very excited to write and share and go deeper. I've woken up in eager anticipation of helping even one person lean into their Fun Size life. So let me take a quick moment here to thank *you* for helping me stay excited about what I get to do in the mornings!

I'm sharing specifically about mornings because, while I personally love mornings, they can also be the most challenging time of day for me. And I know I'm not alone. I know for many people, especially when we are not at our best, mornings can feel unbearable, overwhelming, like the simple act of getting out of bed is a superhuman feat. If you add to that a feeling of loathing for all the things that you have to do that day, it only adds to the weight on your shoulders and chest that keeps you from wanting to get out of that bed. Believe me, I've been there. If I'm not careful about my morning mindset, it's a place I can visit very, *very* easily, even now.

At the points when I was feeling my lowest, I remember that moment of waking up, before all the thoughts really flooded in, was actually a time when I, even if just for a few seconds, felt some relief. That's why, to this day, I cultivate that moment of solitude and connection with my spirit in so many different ways. The more I can anchor myself in that, the more I know I'll be ready for whatever the day has ahead, and I'll be more likely to create good from it than to see or invite the bad.

My little rituals work for me, but yours could be *anything*. I just hope that the above examples prove to you that they don't have to be some kind of time-consuming, high-effort, stress-inducing thing. Looking up into the sky and taking 30 seconds to feel the daylight. Putting your feet in some grass. Making your bed. All of these things and a gazillion more can be *your* anchor that solidifies your morning and makes it special to *you*.

In this case, let's think of Fun Size as indeed small. Because it's those sweet, small moments you choose to use as touchstones that anchor you into one of the many beautiful days in your big, glorious life.

I'M SO NERVOUS (OR AM I?)

I was standing stage left ready to go on for an opera called *Comedy on the Bridge* that I was doing at Berkeley Repertory Theatre. (Yup, an opera. Even now, I'm surprised when I say that. What a crazy ride this career has been.) It was the first time I had ever done an opera, and I was the lead, the soprano ingenue who started the whole show. We had the most incredible artistic team, including two national treasures and a dear and wildly talented friend. The opera had been translated from its original Czech by Tony Kushner, the playwright behind *Angels In America* and the screenwriter behind *Munich*. The designs for the costumes and set were by none other than the glorious author Maurice Sendak (may he rest in peace), and the show was directed by my friend and longtime collaborator Tony Taccone, who was also the artistic director of Berkeley Rep at the time.

Stakes were high, but I felt ready. The rehearsal process was light and fun and challenging in all the right ways, the incredible performers I was sharing the stage with were setting the bar high, my eagerness to try this new challenge in front of an audience was building every day, and I was definitely prepared for performances to begin by the time we got to previews.

But suddenly, when we finally got to that first preview performance, unlike the many plays and musicals I had done up to this point, I found myself consumed by nerves minutes before the show. During the overture, I worried about what could go wrong, how my voice might suddenly crack, how people might not like the show because of something I did at the beginning, and I'd ruin the whole thing.

I'd laugh it off standing there with the stage manager, and every night, I would say some version of, "Ooooh yeah, I should have been a doctor. *That* would have been less stressful," or some such nonsense to brush off the nerves and just get going. This ritual persisted through all of our preview performances, and somehow getting through the show left me, well, relieved but not proud. I felt as though I had dodged a bullet by making it through this show that I had rehearsed for a month and knew full well I was capable of doing. Something about the experience was stealing the joy of performing from me—one of the greatest joys of my life.

Then finally, on the night before our final preview, as we prepared to start the show, for whatever reason, I started thinking about a particular part of the piece that I loved performing and was looking forward to getting to. I stood there for a bit and then realized, *Wait a minute, I'm not nervous, but everything in my physical experience of this moment is exactly the same as it is when I am nervous. Heart's beating a little faster, and I need to keep it chill. My breath wants to be shallow, and I've got a little tiny swarm of butterflies in my stomach flitting around, but this time, all that feels* good.

I had to pause that thought to go on and, ya know, schmact and schming, but that realization stuck with me. The difference between when I was feeling nervous versus excited had to do with the thoughts that I was entertaining—or rather, the outcome I was expecting and the thoughts that followed. When I was expecting things to go poorly, or just trying to prepare myself for them by imagining them all, the nerves and unpleasantness set in. But when I was thinking about how excited and eager I was to see what would happen, to see how the audience would laugh at that particular moment just like I knew they always did, all of a sudden, those physical sensations I was having added up to a very happy and excited Anjali.

"So, Anjali, why are you talking about being nervous or

excited now? I mean, we're well on the journey here; we're rounding third in this book and on this Fun Size Journey map of yours. Why wouldn't you have told us this in the *beginning*?

Ah, yes, that good ol' "Why didn't you tell me about this *before*?!" voice. I know it well. Well, I'll tell ya why: because sometimes (and frankly, I think it's actually more often than we realize), the closer we get to success, the louder those pesky voices in our head begin to scream, "AHHHHHHH! CHANGE IS COMING! It's REALLLL!!!! Let's make sure to tell her all the things that could go wrong because WINTER IS COMING AND THE NIGHT KING IS UNDEFEATABLE!"

(Sorry, couldn't resist throwing in at least one *Game of Thrones* reference here. I mean, talk about epic journeys that could have been aborted at any time if the heroes weren't determined AF. Arya Stark is my spirit animal.)

This is such a well-documented and potentially tragic phenomenon that it has been written about for ages, whether in fiction or non-fiction, with authors warning of the hero's journey too-soon abandoned. In *Think and Grow Rich*,[9] originally written in 1937, Napoleon Hill explains: "More than five hundred of the most successful men this country has ever known, told the author their greatest success came just one step beyond the point at which defeat had overtaken them. Failure is a trickster with a keen sense of irony and cunning. It takes great delight in tripping one when success is almost within reach."

It is so easy to fall into this trap as we're getting closer to the very thing we desire, and so much more tragic if we do, because with the momentum we've built, just like a driver who is suddenly looking exactly where they *don't* want to drive—say, into oncoming headlights or the cliff on the side of the road—we have a much greater chance of crashing and burning rather than staying focused on the road ahead and speeding toward victory. It's another simple thing we're taught in driving school, right? Don't look where you *don't* want to go. But to take that analogy a little further, *do* think about where you're headed and your excitement about getting there. Think about all the good that will come of it, all the joy and satisfaction you will feel. Yes change is coming and it is *good*.

So yes, now that we are here, and you are feeling good and leaning into the journey with full force, I just wanted to hand you one extra tool to give ye olde smackdown to those pesky voices that might pop up. Just a quick little something for you to pop in your pocket the next time you've got something big coming up. To reiterate, instead of preparing yourself for all the things that could go wrong and imagining them in great detail, lean into all the things that could go right. Or at the very least, lean into the possibility that whatever unpredictable things might happen, they could be really fun or surprisingly good.

The future isn't here until it's the present, which means until that moment arrives, whatever you're thinking about is in your imagination anyway. Why not choose the imaginings that feel good and inspire you to be prepared for any eventuality trusting that you've got this rather than imagining your death by embarrassment or failure when neither is actually true yet? Either way, what will happen will happen, so give yourself the feeling of that happy soprano warbling her way through the act for now. You deserve it more than you deserve the fear and anxiety you could create imagining something else. Pick the story that feels better and watch as you get better and better at handling those annoying nerves every time.

WHY NOT CHOOSE THE IMAGININGS THAT FEEL GOOD AND INSPIRE YOU TO BE PREPARED FOR ANY EVENTUALITY TRUSTING THAT YOU'VE GOT THIS RATHER THAN IMAGINING YOUR DEATH BY EMBARRASSMENT OR FAILURE WHEN NEITHER IS ACTUALLY TRUE YET?

YOUR PERSONAL SUPERPOWER

Being a huge fan of comic books, fantasy fiction, science fiction, games, and mythology, I've pondered the word "superpower" for a good portion of my life. The one power we all have that I've seen converted into a superpower time and time again, in people young and old and wise and foolish and happy and sad and from all over the world, is the power of our words. Inside our own minds, on paper, online, in person, on stage, on screen, over radio waves, and in podcasts is the ability to communicate the complexities and intricacies of what we feel and think. It is truly an awesome power—one that can, like any superpower from fiction, both create and destroy.

In *The Four Agreements*, Ruiz starts with agreement number one: Be impeccable with your word. Why? Because your word isn't just a series of letters, it's an energetic call to the Universe, it's a force of creation. And it can light a flame inside someone or snuff it out in an instant. Including yourself.

> "Speak with integrity. Say only what you mean. Avoid using the word to speak against yourself or to gossip about others. Use the power of your word in the direction of truth and love…Find the courage to ask questions and to express what you really want. Communicate with others as clearly as you can to avoid misunderstandings, sadness, and drama. Find yourself and express yourself in your own particular

way. Express your love openly. Life is nothing but a dream, and if you create your life with love, your dream becomes a masterpiece of art."

In the age of the internet where many of us spend more time communicating through smartphones and computers than we do face to face, it has become easier and easier for people to forget that when we put words out into the world, there is someone—or many someones—on the receiving end of that energy. Those words can be poison daggers or they can be loving embraces. And the less and less we connect to the power of those words, the less and less we know the effect we are having on others and on ourselves.

Imagine yourself a superhero along the lines of Captain Marvel or Superman, or a sorcerer like Merlin. Think about the words you have said and the intention with which you have spoken or written them in the last 24 hours. Imagine them as spells or lasers or whatever fantastical imagery resonates with you. Pick something you said and how you said it and really imagine what that moment looks like.

Did you send out a beam of healing energy to someone in distress? Or did you send out a fiery laser that wounded someone on the other end of that Wi-Fi connection? Did the way you spoke to your partner in that last conversation bathe them in love and warmth and give them a shield to go out in the world and sally forth? Or did your words penetrate their skin and leave them vulnerable to more pain and hurt from the world around them?

Part 3: The Home Stretch

Yes, it may sound hyperbolic, but words *are* your superpower, and whether you are a hero or a villain comes not from having that ability, but how you wield it—within yourself, outside yourself. With a hurtful word to someone vulnerable, you can cause unimaginable pain. But with a loving word to someone in need, you can literally save a life. It is not an exaggeration. Choose your words and how you employ them wisely. You have so much power to do great things in the world for so many people, starting with yourself. Take that superpower and make the most of it. I can't wait to hear the tales of how you conquer evil with love, how you empower those who feel powerless, and how you raise people up with the simple act of speaking love and kindness over them. No tights or utility belts necessary.

> WITH A HURTFUL WORD TO SOMEONE VULNERABLE, YOU CAN CAUSE UNIMAGINABLE PAIN. BUT WITH A LOVING WORD TO SOMEONE IN NEED, YOU CAN LITERALLY SAVE A LIFE. IT IS NOT AN EXAGGERATION.

CELEBRATE WHERE YOU ARE

It seems like it's been part of my personality since birth to think that somehow I have to earn my way into being proud of myself. I can remember as early as second grade thinking, "Phew, got an A on that test. But the next one is coming, so I better not get cocky." (Okay it might not have been those exact words because I don't think I even knew what the word "cocky" meant until I heard Han Solo tell Luke Skywalker not to get that way. But the sentiment was definitely there.)

I just wasn't someone who reveled in the success of a moment unless other people around me were doing it with me, like an opening night party or a curtain call. (Come to think of it, that is one tradition that I never realized until now is a perfect example of why it's important to share your wins, too.) It's only recently that I started to understand the value of clocking those moments, and it's precisely because of what I was feeling from forgetting to clock them for so long.

A little while ago I was in a particularly odd and uncharacteristic period of feeling like a quitter because, well, I actually *had* been quitting a lot of things, or not doing them to begin with. I was feeling discouraged and not excited to take on projects, especially when it came to my own health.

After having had that incredible experience I mentioned earlier in this book changing my health habits for the better, somehow at this point, I was finding that I was feeling less and less like doing all of the things that had led me to a healthier and happier place. It was very strange to me. Why had I suddenly become a quitter? What was going on that I couldn't push myself as hard, or loathed doing it? I found myself with an extreme case of what I call "the idon'wannas."

It felt like not only my structured workouts, but also my eating plan and the fun workouts I had started, like getting back into hiking (which I maintain is nature's Prozac and which had brought me so much energy and better moods) now felt like an interminable chore. The joy of doing it was lost on me because I wasn't seeing huge gains anymore, and I felt like I was back to that mindset of running from the fear of something (going back to being out of shape and unhappy with my body) rather than running to something I wanted (the pride I felt in having changed that after so many years).

And then I heard that brilliant fella, Dr. Andrew Huberman (ah yes, him again), talk about why it's important to take the "W."

In short: Because science.

Okay, okay, he's a little more eloquent than that. Allow me to geek out a little (again) because, while I do believe a little in the woo-woo and in a benevolent Universe, I also like to know there's actually a scientific explanation for the thing it took me banging my head against a wall for years to figure out.

I remember this fantastic interview Dr. H did on Tom Bilyeu's *Impact Theory* podcast about growth mindset. When I listened to it, I was caught by what they said about the importance of clocking progress, even the smallest bit. And not in an "everyone gets a medal" way (which I've scoffed at since I was six years old at Arroyo Elementary School; you're not fooling anyone, Mrs. McCleod, coffee is for closers and medals are for winners), but in a way that was logical and truthful enough that one's own brain would accept it.

What's more (and this is the part that made me love listening to Dr. H break it down), neurotransmitters affect our desire to stick with something and our tendency to quit. Essentially, in this interview (and I hope he wouldn't cringe at my simplification of this), he explained that our adrenaline and norepinephrine—commonly known as our fight-or-flight neurotransmitters are excellent for inspiring action. But their effects are limited, and when we have too much of them in our system (usually from too much stress, whether intentional or unintentional, the "good" stress of difficult workouts or the "bad" stress of overdoing it), it can backfire and send us messages of depletion, negativity, and burnout, and increase our desire to quit.

Luckily, one of our "happy" neurotransmitters, dopamine, which is connected to the reward section of our brain, can actually push back on that desire to quit. By giving ourselves the win—not just when we reach the *final* goal, but *all along the way* as we take steps toward it—we can push back on those voices in our brain that are telling us to give up, that it's too hard, that we'll never get there. Or, as Dr. H said:

> "The more you can reward the effort process, the more you can build those reward centers. The key is to not just go through the actions, but the key is that when you hit each of those self-designated milestones that you're setting out for yourself, you have to pause for a moment and tell yourself, 'I'm heading in the right direction. I haven't run the marathon yet, but this is the foundation on which I'm going to lay another foundation on which I'm going to lay anther foundation.'...And those little pulses of dopamine allow you to continue without the depletion that it would normally bring. It feels a little weird...but the ability to control these internal reward schedules is everything."[10]

What made so much sense to me about this (and was such a relief to realize) was that thinking of myself as a quitter missed the full story: Our beautiful brain's neural pathways and our body's intricate system of programming both encourage us to do the very things that are good for us, including the vital step of acknowledging when we are closer to our goal, whatever that goal is. Pushing ourselves nonstop is obviously something that can lead to overtraining, overstressing, and overworking; we know this from the epidemic of burnout we have in the world.

But when we see people who are wildly busy high achievers, who somehow are able to sustain these high levels of performance for prolonged periods of time, it's not because they are alien beings gifted that ability by some outside force. It's likely because they have reinforced behaviors within themselves that allow them to keep going. And a lack of dopamine when we are pursuing a goal means that very thing we are using all our adrenaline and norepinephrine to achieve—whether a 10K race or a stressful deadline—feels farther and farther away, and we begin to question the point of our efforts. We are literally depleting ourselves of energy without replenishing it with one of the easiest all-natural dopamine supplements we can give ourselves: celebration.

I'm not talking about a ticker tape parade, here. As Dr. Huberman said, it isn't about being delusional, but clocking progress is vital. And when you are just starting out, clocking where you are at the beginning and being proud of *starting* is just as important. Giving yourself the credit for taking the very first steps toward something, or for being at the starting line ready to go, at least for me, is vital. *All right, Anj, that's a step in the right direction. You're on your way to something better, something new, something other than this crap you've been feeling.*

Part 3: The Home Stretch

Whether it's taking on a new fitness regimen or starting over after the end of a relationship, you can clock where you are and be proud of yourself for moving forward. Because at any moment, you can say to yourself, "From this day forward...," finish the rest of the sentence, and be proud of being on that journey. Even if it took a seeming failure to get you there, you're there now.

Celebrate where you are. (Hey! I'm on page 265 of this book! It's not the end, but man, we are going in the right direction.)

CAROLINE KINSOLVING
AWARD-WINNING STAGE ACTRESS, YOGA INSTRUCTOR AND CREATOR OF THEATRE AND YOGA FOR GOOD, AND BEAUTIFUL HUMAN
WWW.IAMFUNSIZE.COM/CAROLINEKINSOLVING

"One thing with acting, with anything actually, and actually surfing, this came to mind. I learned when I was 14, and then I didn't do it for years and years and years. And then I moved to Santa Monica, bought myself a surfboard, and I basically would force myself to just go down to the beach every day with the surfboard and paddle out and kind of just sit there and figure it out. Sometimes I would just sit on my board and sometimes I would try to ride some waves and sometimes I would just paddle a lot. And every time I came out of the water—sometimes there would be surfers there looking incredible, sometimes I'd be alone, there were dolphins, it was fantastic—but every time I came out of there, I would force myself to say, 'Progress was made.' Because there were so many voices in my mind going, 'Oh, look at you. I mean, what are you doing? You look like a dead fish.' And I just would go, 'No, I got into the water today,' which is the hardest part, the cold, the whatever, getting into your wetsuit and getting into the water is the hardest part. And I would just say, 'Progress was made, 'cause I did that.' And I think that's true. If you sing a song in public, progress was made, whether you were good or not. If you get in your car and go to an audition, progress was made. Whether you sucked in that audition or you were good in it, progress was made because you had a learning experience. And I think that's really true in the creative world."

WE ARE ALL ARTISTS

Sometimes when I tell people my parents met acting in a play, people look at me with a confused expression, "But I thought they met in medical school?" Yes. That's right. My parents met acting in a play in medical school. (You know, because medical students have so much free time, why wouldn't they also take on doing a play?)

As the story goes, my father was the leading man in an intercollegiate drama troupe that his best friend, Kanthi, ran and directed. They were looking for a young lady to play a role opposite him. My father, much to his friend's chagrin, was vetoing every woman that his friend suggested, and at this point, it was getting ridiculous.

Seeing the frustration on his friend's face, my father declared, "Okay the next girl that walks down those stairs, that'll be the girl." And sure enough, down walked my mother—a petite, fair-skinned, dark-haired beauty in a red sweater and black skirt, or a black sweater and a red skirt. (That fact always seemed to change depending on who was telling the story). Point is, the rest was history.

I know so many who have grown up in families or cultures that seem to value education *or* art, families who travel to Ivy League universities for summer vacation *or* follow acting troupes and music festivals around the country in their Airstream, but sadly, not both. This is why I am incredibly grateful for the good fortune of growing up with and being surrounded by so many people who not only value art but have infused it into their diverse careers and lives.

My mother and father were both brought up in a culture that valued the study of the arts (even if at the time a career in the arts was frowned upon). From the earliest age, I remember both of them treating the world like a canvas to be painted on in their own artistic ways. My mother (in addition to being an excellent actress, by all reports) had such a fine hand at drawing and a beautiful eye for design. Every party she threw had a theme, and she would create the decorations to match.

My 16th birthday party was rife with beautiful handmade mesh butterflies hanging from the ceiling and perched on the tables. My brother's engagement party was lit by a series of floating lotuses in our family pool. When the pool needed to be filled in due to a crack in the foundation, my mother designed a stunning oasis—an epic garden with a waterfall—that served as a haven for our family (and the perfect site for our wedding) in every way.

My mother also went through different craft phases, some more popular than others: the gourmet cooking phase (when, famously in our family lore, after I suggested she relax and we order a pizza for dinner, she turned to me with furrowed brow and determination and said, "We don't order pizza in this family, we make it—*from scratch*"), the puffy paint sweatshirt phase (less appreciated at the time, but oh how I wish those Christmas sweatshirts were still somewhere in our home because I would rock that Rudolph with the jingle bell nose so hard now), several sewing phases (which started well before I was born when she would make beautiful gowns for herself that I then absconded with for costumes for my school plays years later), and of course, interior design, which she is still a master of.

When she writes a birthday card or greeting card of any kind, the poetry of how she expresses her love is so special that I still have a box of cards and letters she has sent me over the years because I can't bear to let any of them go.

My father's artistic expressions were different. Dad was a master of social graces, telling stories with animation and gusto, sharing with enthusiasm and detail what he had recently been reading about or stories from the past, drawing out each moment to keep us all in eager (and sometimes impatient) anticipation. He made everyone around him feel welcome and included, but most of all, he made it safe to *feel*. I now think that is why he was so drawn to acting, because of the freedom we actors are given to express the full range of emotions through storytelling.

Dad's laugh was so big it would light up a room. He would tear up easily at the beauty in the world and at the memory of things from long ago. Even his anger would come out like he was in a Shakespearean play, bold and wild and taken to the fullest degree. And from all reports, he was an artist in the operating room as well, his hands graceful and precise, working with incredible detail and finesse, making the practice of medicine as much an art as anything.

It wasn't just my mother and father, though. There have been so many people who have proven to me that art isn't something only people with careers in the arts have in them or *need* to cultivate. Art is within all of us. Whether it's how you cook a meal at home or spin a conversation waiting tables, how you reimagine a project at work or how you come to an incredible discovery in a laboratory. Whether it's how you sing a song on a stage or to your children when you put them to bed at night.

Think of toddlers playing pretend or drawing pictures at school, singing songs and dancing to music before they even know how to speak. Art is a biological part of our brains and souls. Art is feeling the magic around us that makes the world possible; it's the creativity that inspires technology, industry, space travel, architecture. We all deserve to nurture that part of us no matter how we choose to express it.

I would argue, despite the fact that I *have* chosen to make my living in the arts, those artistic flourishes we put into our lives purely for the joy of it are truly the most vital to keep practicing. Even as a professional creator, I find that if I am not taking time to do some kind of creating purely for myself, my well runs dry, not just in my artistic life but in all aspects of my life.

When Rick's away on tour, I'll write stories for him about Charley and his adventures. When I am home alone, I'll sit at the piano and play a song for myself (however terribly) to feel the vibration of the keys and remember when I first learned to play. I'll learn a song I may never sing onstage because it's beautiful and makes my heart warm. On the rare occasion that I do cook, I'll channel my mother and make sure the dish is as beautiful as it is delicious (although I'm unlikely to ever try to make pizza because, honestly, my mom ruined the curve on that one; hers is *so* good).

When you give yourself the freedom to recognize the artist in yourself, no matter how it comes out, you cultivate a creativity that is uniquely yours. No one feels as you do. No one thinks like you do. No one sees the world through the eyes that you do. In one of the most famous artistic exchanges of all time, visionary choreographer Martha Graham wrote to Agnes de Mille, who was experiencing a confusion and crisis of confidence in her ability to create art that she believed was worthy. De Mille said, "I have a burning desire to be excellent, but no faith that I could be." In her response (the full version of which is framed and prominently displayed in our home), Graham said:

> "There is a vitality, a life force, an energy, a quickening that is translated through you into action, and because there is only one of you in all of time, this expression is unique. And if you block it, it will never exist through any other medium and it will be lost. The world will not have it. It is not your

business to determine how good it is nor how valuable nor how it compares with other expressions. It is your business to keep it yours clearly and directly, to keep the channel open. No artist is pleased."[11]

My friend, whether or not you believe you are an artist, you are. It isn't just about creating art. It is about creating. Period. It is about expressing the unique and wonderful being you are in any way you can. Open the gates to your creativity in any way you can and enjoy playing your life beautifully because it is what you are here to do.*

---

*Some of my favorite books on living artistically include *The War of Art* by Steven Pressfield (which was recently sent to me for the fourth time, this time by a visionary entrepreneur, not an actor or musician or painter or writer—you see?), *Die Empty* by Todd Henry, and *Embrace Your Weird* by Felicia Day. Also very well known in the world is Julia Cameron's *The Artist's Way*, a practice and course in unlocking your own personal creativity and removing those blocks that may have kept you from even seeing it in the first place. These are just a few inspiring pieces though. The list is long and mighty, so explore and find the ones that resonate most with you!

Savoring the Simple Moments

For the first three years that I lived in New York, I lived with my brilliant, giant-hearted cousin Raj, one of the most beautiful humans in my life. Raj is a wildly talented concert pianist, a patient and sublime piano teacher who teaches beginners to advanced students with grace and kindness, a gourmand and gourmet chef who knows how to make something like 60 different chocolate cakes and was responsible for the work of art that was our wedding cake—the list of his talents goes on and on. If you take a trip somewhere he has been, he will regale you with stories of who did what there, what movies were filmed there, what the history of the place is, and other delicious bits to make your enjoyment of the place even greater for the knowing of them.

"This square, Place Furstemburg, is one of my favorite parts of the whole city of Paris where Daniel Day-Lewis is pondering whether to go up to meet Michelle Pfeiffer at the end of *The Age Of Innocence;* the acoustics are perfect and when the classical guitarists used to gather here it was just magical."

"So, Gershwin. George and his brother, Ira, look on this corner, there's a plaque on the building that says they were living there when George wrote 'Rhapsody in Blue.'"

"Ah, Café Lalo...this is where they shot the scene where Meg Ryan and Tom Hanks agree to meet in *You've Got Mail.*"

When I first moved to New York with *Metamorphoses,* I moved into the cozy but well-furnished basement of his two-bedroom condo near Columbia, and when his young piano students would come to take their lessons, I jokingly referred to myself as "the troll who lived under the stairs."

Now, Raj is a person who not only chose an artistic career but lives a truly artistic life, and knows how to relish the finer things, whether you're splurging or on a budget. Before I became a die-hard morning coffee drinker, we shared a beautiful morning ritual of sipping freshly brewed tea each day, courtesy of his seemingly never-ending supply from his (and now my) favorite tea house in Paris, Mariage Freres. Every morning, he would make a pot of fragrant, beautiful tea and we would share that drink together. Marco Polo and Eros were my favorites (although now I've become partial to one called Alexandra David-Neel thanks to its similarity to Indian spiced chai with no milk).

We would start our mornings calmly with the *New York Times* in front of us. (Raj remains the only person I know who still gets a hard copy subscription of the *New York Times* every day, and I love him so much for it.) He would read and I would do the crossword. Then he would go on to practice piano as I continued with my day while listening to the sounds of Schubert, Beethoven, Debussy, and more wafting through the doors of his piano room and coming out of his beautiful antique Steinway piano named Rose.

I know, I know, it sounds (almost laughably) picturesque. And it was. But Raj was also privy to some of the darker times of my life, times when I was so depressed or sad that I couldn't come out from the basement to even make myself eat. Times when even sustaining basic needs felt like a superhuman task, let alone coming upstairs to savor them. Times that I'm sad he had to watch me go through, knowing how much it must have hurt *him* to see me that way. And yet somehow, that tea ritual was always there. No matter how sad I was, it was a life-preserver in a dark, stormy sea.

Thankfully, I came out of that darkness and other dark times after that, and the joyful memory of tea with Raj, along with sitting and listening to his transcendent piano playing, is one of the great simple pleasures of my life. Every time I go to visit, I can't resist sitting down to a cup of tea with him just to feel that beautiful grounding that comes from savoring not just what you eat or drink, but from savoring a moment, a feeling, a memory that no one can take away.

I share this with you now because it's proof that taking the time and focus to savor one simple thing in life that brings you joy, even for a limited period of your life, can keep bringing you joy forever every time you rekindle that memory. When I think of my time living with Raj, I don't remember those depressed days and nights, I remember tea and music and art and love. And as our busy and productive and wonderfully successful and magical lives hurtle us down the path to the finish line, it's still so important to savor those moments whenever we can. Anytime I decide to change it up in the morning and make myself a cup of Mariage Freres, I swear I'm transported back to those days and filled up with love because of my sweet cousin—a man who taught me how to relish the beautiful things in life, no matter how small.

CHARLEY LESSON #6: FOCUS UP, MAMA.

For many years, before Rick and I moved in together, Charley would snuggle up to me while I worked on my computer and diligently try to distract me with his cuteness as I tried to focus. I loved this game: He would use his little snoot to pick up my hand from the computer so I would pet him, forcing me to type with one hand and love on him with the other, or in some extreme circumstances, he would just straight up *sit* on the keyboard when he wanted my attention. Having him get right up in my face with his love and insist that it be returned—*right now*—was a beautiful, adorable reminder of how much he wanted to be the most important part of everything I did.

But as he got older, and after we brought the beautiful presence of my better half into the mix, Charley's insistence turned into a sort of playing hard to get. Now, the second I open up my laptop, he looks at me and *leaves the room*. Mind you, anyone else could be on their computer (he has no problem with Rick typing away) or even on my computer (believe me, I've tried), and he has no problem with it. But when *Mama* opens her laptop, Charley peaces out.

I'll be honest, it's been a little heartbreaking. I miss

PART 3: THE HOME STRETCH

petting his soft fur while I work. But in truth, it's also been a valuable lesson: If you take something or someone for granted, there's always a chance it/they will start to move away or find somewhere else to get that connection. As I said in the section about loving yourself, love is paying attention. I know that Charley can be wooed to sit with me as I type using a lot of treats and bacon, but that's not the important thing to learn here.

Here's Charley's point: Work when you work, play when you play. And *focus* on who you're doing it with, even if it's yourself. Take that time away from the phone or the computer to focus on the people (and doggies) around you. It's so hard to do in today's world, which is why it matters even more. Because the last thing I want is for this doggie to think I love this box of chips and metal more than I love that adorable snoot.

Now hang on, I'm gonna go snuggle with hisself for a few minutes. BRB.

CULTIVATING WONDER (THANK YOU, MS. HUFFINGTON)

I was on my way to shoot a movie in New Orleans and racing through airport security to get to my gate (an uncharacteristic circumstance for me as I usually plan extra time; I relish decompressing alone before a flight, but this particular time, I was in a rush). While I was impatiently waiting for my bags to come through the X-ray machine, I noticed a woman's wallet on the floor beneath the conveyor belt. I reached down, picked it up, and handed it to the security agent, saying, "Someone dropped this. Can you page them or something?" As I collected my bags, I heard over the loudspeaker, "Passenger Arianna Huffington, we have your wallet at security in Terminal 4. Please return to the security area to collect it."

Oh shit. I was stunned because I had been an admirer of Ms. Huffington for years, having seen her on Bill Maher's show numerous times and loving her wit, her intelligence, and her incredible accomplishments. Heartbroken that I couldn't wait to see if she came back to the security area and also hoping I could give her a heads up that the wallet was there, I sent up a flare in the only way I knew might get to her quickly: Twitter.

And off I went to my flight.

Imagine my joy and excitement hours later when I received a reply from Ms. Huffington herself thanking me for helping her and offering to send me a copy of both of her books as thanks. I don't get starstruck often, but as much as I admired her, I was just beside myself to have been able to help. She went even further with her kindness and wrote about the whole event on Twitter, Facebook, her blog, and her Instagram, sharing the gratitude she felt and calling it her Thanksgiving miracle.

In many ways, this was my Thanksgiving miracle, too, because I had no idea how much I needed the book she sent until I received it a week or so later. I immediately began to devour *Thrive: The Third Metric to Redefining Success and Creating a Life of Well-Being, Wisdom, and Wonder*, wildly excited but equally flabbergasted that I hadn't registered until that moment that she had written a book like this. I had known about her book, *The Sleep Revolution,* from her talking about it on Bill Maher a while back, but this book? How had it flown under my radar? Probably just me being scattered and too overwhelmed and busy and focused on other things to clock something that I clearly *should* have known and, and, and...

Before I had a chance to beat myself up as I usually would have for not being able to do and know every single thing, I began to read the book's pages and realized that her very impetus to write this book was her experience of the state I was living in at the time.

In the pursuit of success, which I was ostensibly experiencing much of, I was feeling overwhelmed and fatigued, caring about my health and trying to be healthy but somehow still feeling drained all the time, and most of all, feeling a strange and slowly growing lack of inspiration and joy that made no sense given that I was in the midst of "living the dream." I was shooting two movies back to back, an incredibly popular show I had shot just finished airing to massive success, Rick and I had just had the loveliest visit with my family on the East Coast after not seeing them for far too long. Still, there was a constant niggling thought in the back of my mind saying, "There's no time, hurry up, you're behind, you have to keep working harder, faster, better. Go, go, go."

To explain all of the things I learned from Arianna's book and how it filled my sails and righted my course would take up an entire separate book. But what I *do* want to emphasize here is one of her main points: cultivating *wonder*.

More and more these days, I marvel at the magic of synchronicity, the little bits of magic in the world—like finding Arianna Huffington's wallet and being able to return it to her, and that being my chance to tell someone I admire just how amazing a human they are—that bring things, events, people into our lives at just the right time. The more I cultivate a sense of wonder, the more these magical things seem to happen.

IN OUR HECTIC, RUNAROUND, INFORMATION-OVERLOADED, 24-HOUR-NEWS-CYCLE, NOTIFICATION-LADEN WORLD, ONE OF THE GREATEST CASUALTIES CAN BE OUR SENSE OF WONDER.

In our hectic, runaround, information-overloaded, 24-hour-news-cycle, notification-laden world, one of the greatest casualties can be our sense of wonder. The awe we feel when we take a moment to be truly in the present and marvel at the magnificence of the world around us. The curiosity about nature, humanity, and the world that causes us to ask larger questions about ourselves, about each other, and about what might be beyond the natural realm. The compassion that gives us the urge to reach out to other people and provide comfort, solace, and support to one another, those we know and strangers alike. The wonder that takes us back to how we felt as a child when we saw something in the world and asked that simple question: Why?

There are moments now when I can be sitting still simply thinking about something remarkable in the world—the beauty of the sun glistening off the ocean, the complexity of the human body and how miraculous a machine it is, the ingenuity of a building or a car or some other thing I usually take for granted, the incredible course of events that came together for me to meet, love, and eventually marry my beloved husband, the elegant and loving way my father chose to depart this world in his last days—and tears will come to my eyes.

It's not sadness, it's a sign of something bigger than myself that is filling up my heart so much it needs to come out my eyeballs. And that wonder is a vital part of life for me. It is inspiration, it is comfort, it is gratitude, it is awe. It can adjust the most stressful, busy, frustrating day for me just by moving the kaleidoscope I'm looking through one notch over to see something new.

These are some of my favorite Fun Size ways to cultivate wonder quickly and easily:

- Get out into nature. Skip the headphones and keep the cell phone in your pocket. There have been more times than I can count that I've been able to unravel the spaghetti-like thoughts racing through my brain just by being out and focusing on the beauty of trees or sky or even the ground below me. (It's one of the many reasons I feel blessed to live in Los Angeles, where you can have city and nature very easily within the same hour.)

- Play with your pet if you have one, or just a friendly one you meet. Really focus on how present and connected that little creature is. I swear, dogs have the answers to everything somewhere in their precious little souls.

- Connect with a stranger in kindness and service. It could just be smiling at a person as you walk down the street or waving at someone as you drive by. And yes, sometimes you may get strange looks because people aren't so used to that in our world, but you'd be surprised how many people will immediately feel a jolt of something lovely and smile or wave back. A smile truly can change someone's day.

- Read a book for no other reason than enjoyment. Not for work, not with goals in mind, just to go on the adventure. My favorites for these purposes are usually fantasy or science fiction—something that takes me out of this world for a few moments (or hours) to get my brain wondering about the possibilities that are limited only by my own imagination.

- Get a new perspective on life (literally) by sitting or lying down or standing in a part of your home you rarely or never do. We've lived in our small but mighty home for going on four years, and I still find new spots to sit in and look at the rest of the room or to lie down on the floor at a different angle than I have before. You can absolutely try this now (if you're somewhere safe to do it)! Get up and move somewhere in your home you haven't sat before, and just take a minute or so (or more if you'd like) to take in what the room looks like before coming back to this book. I find some of the most random and wonderful thoughts and ideas I've had come from that simple change of environment. You don't have to go on a walkabout or vacation to get that new perspective. (My brilliant playwright friend, D Tucker Smith, uses this to great effect in a scene in her play, *Roof of the World,* which I had the great joy of bringing to life with her in 2016. I always loved that the character and I both had the same habit of lying on the floor.)

- *Literally* wonder about something. In any of the above environments, entertain the words, "I wonder…" and finish the sentence. Give yourself the gift of not running to Google immediately for the answer. Let yourself muse on something you might have taken for granted. You can do this any time of day or night, in any environment. It's also a beautiful way to come up with innovations, ideas for stories, plays, shows, or just about anything you may be creatively stuck on.

- Give. Just like that brief moment when I saw Arianna Huffington's wallet and stopped to grab it even though I was late, you'd be surprised how much of a difference being just a little less focused on yourself can make in the world around you *and* in your own world. That moment when you stop and wait to hold the door for someone who is a few steps farther away, that time you help someone who is clearly struggling with directions as they stand on the subway platform, that moment you offer a cup of coffee or water to that worker who is working outside your building—these opportunities for giving have the power to take us out of ourselves and make us a part of the world around us, and to fill us with the connectedness that says, "You are you, uniquely you, but you are never alone." That, right there, is a thing of wonder.

And thanks again, Arianna. My book is dog-eared, underlined, written in, and well-loved, and my life was changed for the better thanks to you.

PART 3: THE HOME STRETCH

CHLOE HOLLINGS

ACTRESS (OVERWATCH, ON THE VERGE), AUTHOR (FUCK LES RÉGIMES), HOST OF MAIS OUI/A TASTE OF HONEY, AND ALL-AROUND LOVELY PERSON
WWW.IAMFUNSIZE.COM/CHLOEHOLLINGS

"I try to get my inspiration in nature. I try to look at how nature works. And there is no such thing as a flower that is just this color or a fruit that, when you buy a hundred of them, they will all look the same. We evolve, we change with the seasons. I change all the time based on, like, how tired I am or what my hormones are doing or what my love life is like. And we should value that instead of trying to just repress it. Because at the end of the day, what we love the most is people who are on their own thing, that's their own unique thing. That's what we're drawn to everyday. So why won't we allow that for ourselves?"

THERE IS NO WASTED TIME

Perfection is a myth and I ain't no unicorn—unless you ask my husband, who likes to tell me on the reg that I *am* a unicorn. Yes, feel free to roll your eyes at how cute that is; I would have, too, before I met him. But seriously, even after all my talk in this book about how to Fun Size your life, I do struggle with a lot of it. In fact, I'm starting to wonder if I really wrote this book for myself. The good news is, now the struggle tends to give me more insight to help myself *and* others. So, to illustrate, here's one of my more recent highly imperfect moments and how I decided to use it for the better.

Not too long ago, I was having one of those nights, well, early mornings: mind racing, can't stop the not-so-helpful thoughts, lying in bed unable to sleep but not wanting to give up just yet on the possibility of sleeping. Usually at this point, I would grab my earbuds and listen to my favorite meditation (Relaxing – Take 5, with strings, by David Rowan, if anyone's asking) and, nine times out of 10, would fall into a comfortable snooze without much ado.

But this morning, I was laying on my side, firmly ensconced between a snoozing dog curled up against my stomach and my fast-asleep hubs with his arm so far around me he could embrace me *and* the pup in one move. There was no moving without creating a deep disturbance in the Force, and I wasn't about to wake either of my boos from their nighttime revels.

So instead, I was stuck with my thoughts, and I figured, hey, I'm writing this book right now, lemme just take a little dive into this spiral and see what's what. Maybe I can find something helpful worth sharing with people while I drive myself nuts.

Here's where it went:

> *Ugh. I can't believe how much money I've spent this year getting my business going. I mean, if I hadn't been all ambitious and wanting more, if I'd just been satisfied with what I had, I probably could have had so much in savings now. Instead, I've got a business loan that I don't know when I'm going to be able to repay because who knows if this business is gonna work out. And the book? Ugh, I was so excited to write it, to share it, but look how much time I've spent doing it, and look at how much time I wasted not doing it. I mean, what the hell, Anj, you've had this idea for, what, three years? People have been telling you to write for ages and it took you until now? I mean, your horoscope even told you when the perfect time to do it was and you blew that off for, like, two years, and now that's changed. If you had just done this when you were also working more and flush, or done it earlier in the pandemic, it would have been the perfect time, but you're doing it now? When you're supposed to be looking for more work and making more money? Why are you always so behind?*

Ohhhhhhhkay, that was enough of that spiral, so I stopped it right there on that big ol' golden nugget of a limiting belief that I knew had to go away immediately. Happily, at that same moment, my alarm went off, so, yup, no sleep was happening, but at least now I had something to work with.

I've started to step outside of myself a lot when I'm having these negative spiral moments (in-spiral-ing) and choose to let them go a little further. I look for the thought that is causing me to dig that hole deeper and deeper because I know, a lot of the time, there's a big piece of fool's gold I'm digging for that needs to be excavated and tossed out. Gotta get rid of that crap before I can find the real golden nugget and have the proverbial, "There's gold in them thar hills!" moment.

So after said reverie, I got up and found my sweet little overactive brain was now, as a little side hustle, working on serving up all the ways I had wasted time in my life and poking at one of my Achilles' heels: the feeling that I'm behind and have wasted time and now there's no time to be wasted so I have to rush and panic and move faster. As I calmly brushed my teeth (because again, I was letting all this go on "for research"), my mind presented memory after memory—the six-and-a-half year relationship I was in that should have ended after the third date, the months and months over the course of so many years I spent loathing myself and feeling so sad that I couldn't enjoy any of my successes, the many Thanksgivings and Christmases I spent with my brother, sister-in-law, cousin, niece, and nephew, incredible family times, that I hadn't been able to soak in and enjoy because I was thinking of all the other places I should be instead, never realizing how special it was to be able to be a family like that and how much I should be treasuring the time.

And then, another memory popped up, one that pops up relatively frequently but seemed a little out of place. It was a random morning from my junior year of high school as we were sitting at our desks getting ready for Mrs. Chen's calculus class. I had hefted my giant backpack onto my chair and was huffing and puffing in frazzled frustration, and my friend, Barbra Tibbles, happily asked, "Hey, how ya doing?" to which I replied, "Ugh, I'm just having the worst morning. I'm so far behind, I've been running late for hours and I just feel like I can't catch up." Barbra looked at me like I had three heads and asked, "How is that possible? It's 7 a.m.!"

I don't remember what happened after that. Probably me muttering something to myself about how she couldn't understand how stressed I was and how much I had to do as we all sat down to focus on whatever mathematical genius was to be bestowed on us that day. But the fact that I was feeling that *at 16* has somehow stuck with me. (Now, I will maintain that if I had to do high school again these days, I don't think I'd survive it because I see how much our kids have to do and deal with and study and work, and it makes me tired just watching them. But even back in ye olde tyme, there was a lot to be done.)

The problem, however, wasn't just the circumstances. It was the mindset I had of time scarcity. The conversation with Barbra was not unlike one I've had with my husband many, many times in the last year. Poor thing will barely have opened his eyes, and I'll be racing into the bedroom, muttering something along the lines of ,"Ugh, running late again, no matter how early in the morning I wake up, I just can't seem to get anything done and I'm so behind."

Yeahhhhhhhh, this is a deep and ongoing belief.

The truth is, there is no wasted time *except* the time you spend running around thinking you have no time. *Except* the time you spend not living your life and wishing you were somewhere else. *Except* the time you are so far in the past or present that you can't possibly see or enjoy what's going on around you. The only thing that telling yourself you've wasted time does is make you panic. And that's a waste of time. Stop, adjust your course, and get going. No need to race and freak out. Just get back on track and go.

To clarify, I'm not asking you to blow off reality. I'm telling you to actually be *in* reality. It may seem like conflating the two concepts here, but I believe that the feeling of not enough time and thinking that you've wasted time doing something are very much bosom buddies. Time scarcity and regret go very much hand in hand. They are the product of so many practices that I am unfortunately very accustomed to using, including being inflexible with plans.

You've heard the John Lennon lyrics, "Life is what happens when you're busy making other plans"? If you're too busy telling yourself how things should be or should have been, there's no room to see how things are. And in this very moment, there might be something miraculous you're missing that would bring you precisely to the destination you were trying to get in the first place—or even better, to somewhere you didn't imagine you *could* get to but that you very much want to be.

If I hadn't gone through the six-and-a-half years of relationship experience I had with Mr. Not Right before meeting Rick, and had at least started to heal and learn from it, there's no *way* I would have been ready for the insane course of adventures and pitfalls that brought us together, and that we have faced together now. It's precisely *because* of that so-called wasted time that I know exactly how valuable what we have is. It's precisely because of the memory of all those holidays when I couldn't bring myself to be present that I found myself on the verge of happy tears so many times during the last time I got to spend Thanksgiving with my family back East.

> **IF YOU'RE TOO BUSY TELLING YOURSELF HOW THINGS SHOULD BE OR SHOULD HAVE BEEN, THERE'S NO ROOM TO SEE HOW THINGS ARE.**

There is no wasted time *if* you stay in it—even the crap, even the dark times. Because whatever you are present for is what you'll remember, whether it's a sad and stressed conversation with your friend 30 years ago before calculus class, a lesson you finally learned when you stood for what you were worth and ended a difficult relationship, or a warm memory of your friend Cathleen's pumpkin spice gingerbread muffins that you brought to Thanksgiving and enjoyed with wine and laughter and joy with your family. Each moment has its importance. Each one has a place in your story. None of it was wasted time.

Anjali Bhimani

ELLE NEWLANDS
VOICE ACTRESS (APEX LEGENDS, WORLD OF WARCRAFT), EQUESTRIAN GODDESS, SELF-PROCLAIMED "SASSY SCOTTY," AND COMPASSIONATE AND CARING FRIEND
WWW.IAMFUNSIZE.COM/ELLENEWLANDS

"The truth of it is, you can only be where you're at; nothing is wasted time because the more life you live, the more knowledge becomes unlocked. And the more knowledge that becomes unlocked, that gives you the ability to look back and go, 'Wow, I wasted time.' Because at the time when you were 'wasting your time,' you didn't have the knowledge. You were doing the best with the knowledge that you had at that time. And that's the beauty of that time that you spend; potentially it's time when you were heartbroken, you got hurt, you were in a bad place, whatever it is. It's not a waste of time because it's time that took you to this current space for you to go, 'Wow. I feel different now. And I want different things.' And that's the whole point in life."

WAIT A SECOND. IS THIS...HAPPINESS?

In 2017, a few months after my father's passing, I was doing a play called *Orange* at the South Coast Repertory theatre in Costa Mesa. The show (beautifully conceived and written by Aditi Kapil) was set entirely in the very county I grew up in, and it was such a love letter to my teenage years that every night when I drove down from Los Angeles and back, it was like a visit to my childhood. Of course, when I was a child and a teenager, I was filled with angst and stress and fear and all the itinerant challenges of growing up. Visiting at this time in my life, after I had just gone through the period of truly tumultuous events I shared at the beginning of this book, was oddly peaceful and therapeutic.

One night, as I was making the hour-and-a-half-long drive back home to Los Angeles after the show, I was listening to a podcast in the car when I suddenly noticed something. Something very, very odd.

There were no voices in my head.

No voices of judgment telling me I was doing something wrong, no voices of worry telling me I had so much to do, no voices of frustration or disdain or "you're not enough," in fact, no voices at all. All I was hearing and processing were the words of the speaker and interviewee on the podcast. I was present, relaxed, and open.

Is this what happiness feels like?

I remember once my dear mentor Cathleen telling me, "I have a secret to tell you. After years of "drahhhhhma", the ups and downs, the emotional swings and roller coasters we take when we aren't really able to understand how to clear our emotions, after years of that, of that habit, happiness can honestly feel...a little boring."

She wasn't saying it as a bad thing, but more to warn me that happiness might actually feel a little uncomfortable at first, like, "This is too easy; this can't possibly be it," uncomfortable. But in that moment, that feeling of peace, that feeling of maybe everything isn't perfect but all is right with my world, I realized it was the first time in years— maybe even decades—that I had clocked that I wasn't fighting a war with myself in my head. The banners had been taken down, the soldiers had left the battlefield, and there was a peace that felt just...simple.

I'm so grateful that in that moment, I had the wherewithal to note the feeling because, in truth, it was somewhat fleeting. Still, I knew from that moment on that it was that simplicity, that ease, that peace that was the very thing I had been pursuing for so long. And it didn't require money or success or any kind of outside input telling me that I had a *right* to be happy. All that I had in that moment was me— and no voices telling me that "just me" wasn't enough.

To this day, I think back to that moment often, not with

yearning but with recognition. Because when we practice something—including our own feelings—we can create more of them simply through clocking them and allowing them to be. Rehearsing them, if you will. I have been able to create more and more moments of that peaceful happiness since then, again, not because of outside influences, but because I have learned to embrace that state of being as an, "I am," not an, "I wish I was," or a "Someday I'll be."

I am.

And while circumstances and frustrations and struggles and challenges will come up and shift me off that feeling (because life), I know that place lives inside me always. I know I can visit it any day, any moment the more and more I recognize it, practice it, and invite it into my home. I spent far too many years romancing dark or painful thoughts and feelings. Not just romancing them, I would wine them and dine them and take them out to dinner, the way I insisted they were real. But learning to treat simple (and occasionally boring) happiness with that same love and reverence has been a joy I can't explain. And a relief.

If I could buy everyone I meet a ticket to that station, I would. Instead, to accomplish that for you and for me however I can, I am writing this book.

Don't be alarmed if when you get to your goals, or on the way there, or even in moments when you feel like life isn't going your way, you find these moments of peaceful, boring happiness. They are real and true and yours to own. You can always go back to struggling, to challenges, to the ups and downs of life. They will always be there. But just remember that delicious, occasionally boring happiness is there, too. Feel free to sit in it and believe in it because it is yours to have.

SOME FINAL THOUGHTS (JUST FOR NOW; YOU CAN'T GET RID OF ME THAT EASILY)

> "I AM NOT AFRAID OF STORMS, FOR I AM LEARNING HOW TO SAIL MY SHIP."
> — LOUISA MAY ALCOTT

Life is unpredictable and beautiful and scary and wonderful and heartbreaking and wildly exciting, and no matter how hard we may try to avoid it, there will be moments of pain and struggle amidst the joys and successes.

I hope some of the stories and perspectives and random giggles in this book are useful as you keep surfing the waves of your world. I find that the more I experience and just plain survive, let alone thrive, the more I realize it's all going to be okay, even in the most painful of moments, because it always has been.

And when it feels like it may never be okay, please know that you aren't alone. Not in your world, not in the world. Thanks to the internet, we have access 24/7 to other people all over the globe, and if you can't reach that one person you wish you could connect with, there are multitudes of people out there who, despite not knowing you, would happily help you and cheer you on in your pursuit of a big, beautiful, Fun Size life.

I'm handing over the flashlight for now so you can keep journeying on your way. But all around you every day, you can find me and others to celebrate you, whether you are traveling the world or sitting at your computer. You are Fun Size. You are built for the best life *you* can imagine. It's your vision, your creation, and we're all here in the audience ready to give you that standing ovation as you create it. Go shine.

With love and hugs and puppy belly rubs,

Anjali (and Charley Boo)

ACKNOWLEDGEMENTS

If left to my own devices, the acknowledgements for this book would be just as long as the book itself. Since this book has so much of my life in it, it feels like everyone who has contributed to my world in any way belongs here. Editing this section is probably the hardest part of the editing process because I want to include so very many people, but if I try to get them all in, chances are I will somehow manage to leave out someone (or several someones) that I will hate myself later for omitting. So instead of listing everyone, please know that if you are someone dear to me and you are somehow not on this page, you're definitely in my thoughts and heart.

As far as this book and the folks responsible for making it happen, many thanks (in no particular order):

To my right-hand man (still working on a better title for you), Denis Shepherd, without whom this book would likely have remained in my head and not on the page for months (if not years) longer; to my editors, Lauren Terrell, Chantel Hamilton, and Jessica Sherer, for their expertise, patience, encouragement, and positivity dealing with this first-time author; to Sandy Kreps for making sure the visual experience of reading this book was as fun as I imagined it to be; to my manager, Caleigh Vancata, for making sure I never had to sacrifice living a big life for having a satisfying career or vice versa; to my dear friend, Marisha Ray, for not only being a constant inspiration to me as a creator and a human but also for contributing her words and brilliance in the foreword, and my equally beloved Matthew Mercer for his creative brilliance and leading by example as a person, a friend, a storyteller, and a creator of wondrous experiences that expand my heart every time I get to share in them; to Vivian Truong, my SuperRisu, who made writing this book even more fun imagining the adorable art I knew she would come up with for it (and more); to the guests on I Am Fun Size and the wise friends who allowed me to use their words in this book; to my sweet Ceddy Lopez, who was one of the very first people to suggest I write this book and one of my most relentless champions in this endeavor and more; to B Dave Walters without whose encouragement, wisdom, knowledge, and all-around wonderfulness I wouldn't have been able to put together the Kickstarter that filled me with even more inspiration to get this book out into the world; and once again, to the Kickstarter community that rallied behind this project and not only gave their financial support but also further inspired me with their excitement for this project.

Acknowledgements

Special thanks to the following supporters for their extra generous contributions to this project:

Parvesh Cheena	Q Fortier
Eric Politzer	Lachlan Finlayson
Ashley Earl	Evan Daleu Heuker
Lindsay Rucker	Louisa Pragst
Joe Padron	Melissa Huber
Desmond Li	Erin Chambers
Jessica Smith	Michael & Natasha Graziano
Adam Breon	Adam Ferguson
Lester Acosta	Ariana Mazer
Yen-Shyang Tseng	Dan Gordon
Victoria Dutcher	Patch Perryman
Mike Zeller	Justin Bohm
Mike Urano	Owynn Taylor
Niti Merchant	Binita Donohue
Sven Nielsen	David Krambeck
Bill Neubauer	Jon Peck & Alena Perout

And yes, again, to Rick—somehow, despite being a full foot and four inches taller than I am, you make me feel bigger than anyone ever has. Thank you for Fun Sizing my life.

NOTES

PART 1

1. Peter M. Gollwitzer, Paschal Sheeran, Verena Michalski, and Andrea E. Seifert. (2009). "When Intentions Go Public: Does Social Reality Widen the Intention-Behavior Gap?" *Psychological Science* 20, no. 5 (2009): 612-618, https://doi.org/10.1111/j.1467-9280.2009.02336.x

2. Michelle Obama. "It's Okay to Not Have It All." Posted December 12, 2019. Filmed during the Obama Foundation Leaders: Asia-Pacific Program, Kuala Lumpur. Video, 7:59. https://www.youtube.com/watch?v=qHyQd1Xpm4w

3. Jim Kwik, *Limitless: Upgrade Your Brain, Learn Anything Faster, and Unlock Your Exceptional Life* (Carlsbad, CA: Hay House, Inc., 2020), 11-13.

4. Greg McKeown, *Essentialism: The Disciplined Pursuit of Less* (New York: Crown Business, 2014), 86.

PART 2

5. Don Miguel Ruiz and Janet Mills, *The Four Agreements: A Practical Guide to Personal Freedom* (San Rafael, CA: Amber-Allen Publishing, 1997.

6. Todd Henry, *Die Empty: Unleash Your Best Work Everyday* (New York: Portfolio/Penguin, 2015), 52.

7. Caroline Myss, Sacred Contracts: Awakening Your Divine Potential (New York: Harmony Books, 2003), 390.

PART 3

8. Daniel Goleman, Emotional Intelligence: Why It Can Matter More Than IQ (New York: Bantam Books, 2006).

9. Napoleon Hill, Think and Grow Rich (Shippensburg, PA: Sound Wisdom, 2017), 13.

10. Tom Bilyeu, "This Neuroscientist Shows You the Secrets to Obtaining a Growth Mindset: Andrew Huberman," May 21, 2020, on Impact Theory, video, 54:55, https://www.youtube.com/watch?v=OGa_jt3IncY.

11. Agnes De Mille, *Martha: The Life and Work of Martha Graham* (New York: Random House, 1991).

ABOUT THE AUTHOR

Anjali Bhimani is an award-winning actor whose career spans across stage and screen from Broadway to feature films, television, video games, animation, and original online content. She is most proud of her leading roles as partner-in-crime to her husband, Rick, and as mother of Charley the Best Dog, and can be seen driving or walking the pup while wearing her hot rollers on the streets of West Hollywood, where they all currently reside.

Her television and film credits include *Ms. Marvel, Special, Crazy Ex-Girlfriend, Marvel's Runaways,*

About the Author

Modern Family, The Sopranos, and many more. She is well known to gaming and animation audiences for her roles as Symmetra in *Overwatch,* Rampart in *Apex Legends,* the proud and feisty Miriam on *UnDeadwood,* the noble Fy'ra Rai on *Exandria Unlimited* by Critical Role, and the strong-headed sniper Stingray in *We're Alive: Frontier* on the popular YouTube channel *Geek and Sundry.*

She earned her degree in theatre from Northwestern University's highly acclaimed theatre school, with a certificate in musical theatre, and spent years performing across the country in top organizations such as Second Stage, Manhattan Theatre Club, The Goodman Theatre, Berkeley Repertory Theatre, The McCarter Theatre, The Huntington Theatre Company, and more. She has collaborated with theatre luminaries such as director Mary Zimmerman, writer Tony Kushner, and legendary composers A.R. Rahman and Andrew Lloyd Webber. She was an original cast member of the Tony-nominated *Metamorphoses* on Broadway, which won the Drama Desk Award for Outstanding Play.

She is the creator of *I Am Fun Size,* a YouTube series in which she shares her experiences and interviews other well-known performers to help people find their fullest lives through life's challenges.

Anjali can be found on Twitter, Instagram, and YouTube at @sweeetanj and on Facebook at Facebook.com/anjalibhimani. You can also keep up with Anjali by joining her email list at www.AnjaliBhimani.com.

FUN SIZE NOTES

A LITTLE SPACE FOR MORE GOODIES OF YOUR OWN!